Knitted
ANIMAL TOYS

25 KNITTING PATTERNS FOR ADORABLE ANIMAL DOLLS

LOUISE CROWTHER

DAVID & CHARLES

www.davidandcharles.com

CONTENTS

INTRODUCTION

Welcome to my collection of animal toys, all knitted with one thing in mind: to make them irresistible. We all have a special person in our lives who would love one of these little characters, even if it's ourselves! If you can't choose between a smart fox, or a cheeky raccoon, you could always make them all...

In this book I have gathered all the information you will need from yarn choice to finishing techniques, and kept the patterns concise and clear to make the creation of each animal as enjoyable to knit as the finished toy is to give.

The patterns in this book are designed for you and your friends and family to enjoy and are for private use only. I can't wait to see photos of your knitted animal toys! Share them using the hashtag #knittedanimaltoys so that I can enjoy looking at your creations and you can take a look at everyone else's too.

Whatever you choose to knit, I hope that you enjoy the process and cherish your finished animal toy as much as I have loved designing and creating them.

TOOLS AND MATERIALS

YARN

Cotton yarn has always been my favourite yarn for toys. I love the look and feel of cotton, it is non-allergic for most people, incredibly robust and stands up well to being played with.

The animals in this book have all been made using Scheepjes Stonewashed yarn which is a sport weight 78% cotton/22% acrylic mix yarn. Sport weight is slightly thicker than 4-ply but thinner than DK, also sometimes referred to as 5-ply yarn.

Although I recommend using the above yarn to achieve the same look and feel as my animals, the patterns will work just as well with other sport weight yarn. When substituting yarns you need to look for ones with a similar tension/gauge on the ball band as the ones recommended (see below for ball band information).

BALL BAND INFORMATION:

SCHEEPJES STONEWASHED

Available in balls of 50g (1¾oz) = 130m (142yd)

Tension: 24 stitches and 32 rows for a 10 x 10cm (4 x 4in) tension square using 3-3.5mm (US 2½–US 4) needles.

NEEDLES

The animals are all made flat on a pair of straight needles; I like the structure this gives the animals and find working Intarsia and stuffing the toys much easier this way.

You will need a pair of 2.75mm (US 2) straight needles to knit the animals '(and a pair of 3mm (US 2½) double-pointed needles to make Ella the Unicorn), but you may find you need to adjust your needle sizes to achieve the correct tension/gauge.

BUTTONS

For the animals' eyes I have used 10mm (½in) diameter buttons.

Safety note – *Don't use safety eyes, buttons, beads or glass eyes on toys for children under three years old as they are a potential choking hazard.*

STUFFING

I recommend a synthetic high-loft polyester toy filling for stuffing these animals. It is lovely and soft, holds its shape well and is hand or machine washable on a cool delicates cycle. When stuffing your animal use small pieces, roll and manipulate the body parts in your hands to spread the stuffing evenly and ensure a smooth shape. Tease out any lumps using a blunt tapestry needle carefully inserted through the knitting in the gap between stitches.

BASIC KIT

In addition to the things on the 'You Will Need' lists in the patterns, these are the other items you need to complete the animals. The following is a basic guide:

- Cable needle
- Tapestry needle
- Stitch holders
- Stitch markers
- Removable stitch markers
- Waste yarn
- Sewing needle and thread
- Long sewing needle
- Scissors
- Toy stuffing
- Blocking pins

WASHING

If made using the recommended yarn and stuffed with synthetic toy filling, these animals can either be washed by hand or on a gentle cool cycle in your washing machine. I would recommend reshaping the animals whilst still damp.

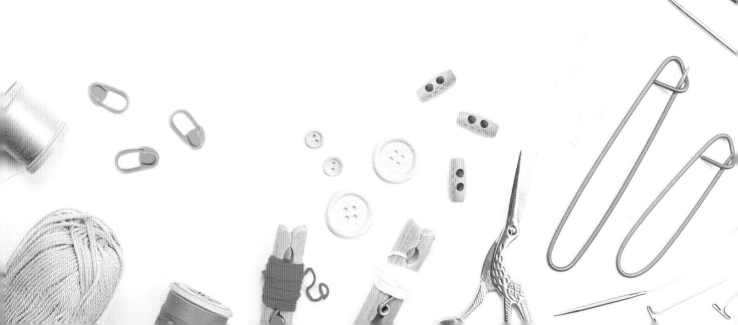

ABBREVIATIONS

CDD	Central double decrease: slip 2 stitches together knitwise, K1, pass the 2 slipped stitches over
dpn(s)	Double-pointed needle(s)
K	Knit
K2tog	Knit 2 stitches together
K3tog	Knit 3 stitches together
Kfb	Knit 1 stitch through front loop, then knit through back loop
kw	Knitwise
LH	Left-hand
M1	Make 1 stitch: from the front, lift loop between stitches with left needle, knit into back of loop
m1a	Make one away: create a loop by placing right thumb over working yarn, rolling it behind, under, then back up in front of yarn. Place loop onto RH needle
m1l	Make 1 left: from the front, lift loop between stitches with left needle, knit into back of loop
m1pl	Make one purlwise left: from the front, lift loop between stitches with left needle, purl into back loop
m1pr	Make one purlwise right: from the back, lift loop between stitches with left needle, purl into front loop
m1r	Make 1 right: from the back, lift loop between stitches with left needle, knit into front of loop
P	Purl
P2tog	Purl 2 stitches together
P3tog	Purl 3 stitches together
PCDD	Purl central double decrease: slip 1 knitwise, slip 1 knitwise, pass both slipped stitches back onto LH needle, slip 2 stitches together through the back loops and pass them back onto LH needle once again. Purl 3 stitches together

pm	Place marker
PSSO	Pass slipped stitch(es) over
pw	Purlwise
RH	Right-hand
Rnd(s)	Round(s)
rpt	Repeat
rs	Right side
sl1	Slip 1 stitch purlwise
sm	Slip marker
SSK	Slip 2 stitches knitwise one at a time, knit together through back loops
SSP	Slip 2 stitches knitwise one at a time, purl together through back loops
SSSK	Slip 3 stitches knitwise one at a time, knit together through back loops
SSSP	Slip 3 stitches knitwise one at a time, purl together through back loops
St(s)	Stitch(es)
Stocking stitch	Knit all stitches on right side rows, purl all stitches on wrong side rows
ws	Wrong side
wyib	With yarn in back
wyif	With yarn in front
YO	Yarn over

ESSENTIAL NOTES

The best way to avoid potential muddles is to start off correctly, and to be armed with advance knowledge of any particular techniques a knitting pattern might ask for. Please do read the following notes before you begin – they apply to all the patterns and they're not called essential for nothing!

FINISHED SIZE
All of the animals are approximately 40cm (16in) tall (excluding ears).

TENSION
29 sts and 47 rows to 10 x 10cm (4 x 4in) over stocking stitch using 2.75mm (US 2) needles.

FOR ALL PATTERNS...

• Cast on using the Long tail cast-on (double cast-on) method (see Techniques: Casting On and Stitches). Leave long tails when you cast on and cast off to sew the parts together, this will make your life easier when sewing up the animals.

• Use Mattress stitch (see Techniques: Casting On and Stitches) for sewing up seams (unless stated otherwise) and weave in ends as you go.

• Use the Intarsia technique (see Techniques: Colourwork) for changing yarn across a row; the different yarn colours within a row are indicated in brackets: (A) = use Yarn A, (B) = use Yarn B.

• If you find the central increase stitches on the animal's head too tight to manage, wrap the yarn twice around the needle when knitting or purling the centre stitch on the row below, dropping this extra wrap before making the first central increase on the next row.

• Always slip markers as you come to them unless otherwise stated.

STANDARD BODY PARTS

All of the animals are a standard size and shape, and most feature the same basic bodies, arms and legs. The standard patterns for these body parts are given here and referenced throughout the book. Yarn details and any alterations to the patterns are provided with the instructions for each animal, but please feel free to mix and match the different body part styles and vary the colours to create your own unique animals too!

Before you start, please read the Essential Notes at the beginning of this book.

BODY

PLAIN (PHOTO 1)
Using Yarn A and 2.75mm straight needles, cast on 8 sts.
Starting at base:
Row 1 (ws): Purl.
Row 2: [K1, M1] to last st, K1. (15 sts)
Row 3: Purl.
Row 4: [K2, M1] to last st, K1. (22 sts)
Row 5: Purl.
Row 6: [K3, M1] to last st, K1. (29 sts)
Row 7: Purl.
Row 8: [K4, M1] to last st, K1. (36 sts)
Row 9: Purl.
Row 10: [K5, M1] to last st, K1. (43 sts)
Row 11: Purl.
Row 12: [K6, M1] to last st, K1. (50 sts)
Row 13: Purl.
Row 14: [K7, M1] to last st, K1. (57 sts)
Row 15: Purl.
Row 16: [K8, M1] to last st, K1. (64 sts)
Row 17: P20, K10, P4, K10, P20. (The knit stitches on this row mark the leg positions.)

Rows 18-37: Stocking stitch 20 rows.
Row 38: K1, K2tog, K17, CDD, K18, CDD, K17, SSK, K1. (58 sts)
Rows 39-47: Stocking stitch 9 rows.
Row 48: K1, K2tog, K15, CDD, K16, CDD, K15, SSK, K1. (52 sts)
Rows 49-55: Stocking stitch 7 rows.
Row 56: K1, K2tog, K13, CDD, K14, CDD, K13, SSK, K1. (46 sts)
Rows 57-61: Stocking stitch 5 rows.
Row 62: K1, K2tog, K11, CDD, K12, CDD, K11, SSK, K1. (40 sts)
Rows 63-67: Stocking stitch 5 rows.
Row 68: K1, K2tog, K9, CDD, K10, CDD, K9, SSK, K1. (34 sts)
Rows 69-71: Stocking stitch 3 rows.
Row 72: K1, K2tog, K7, CDD, K8, CDD, K7, SSK, K1. (28 sts)
Rows 73-75: Stocking stitch 3 rows.
Row 76: [K1, K2tog] to last st, K1. (19 sts)
Row 77: Purl.
Row 78: K2tog to last st, K1. (10 sts)

Cut yarn leaving a long tail. Using a tapestry needle, thread tail through the stitches left on needle and pull up tight to gather stitches.

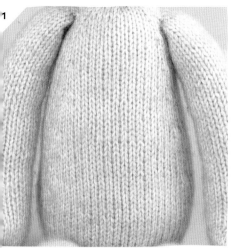
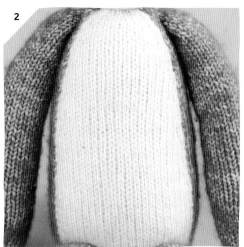
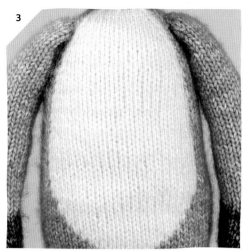

CONTRAST FRONT 1 (PHOTO 2)

Using Yarn A and 2.75mm straight needles, cast on 8 sts.

Rows 1-17: As Rows 1-17 of Standard Body – Plain.

Row 18: (A) K21, (B) K22, (A) K21.

Row 19: (A) P21, (B) P22, (A) P21.

Rows 20-37: Rpt last 2 rows 9 more times.

Row 38: (A) K1, K2tog, K16, K2tog, (B) SSK, K18, K2tog, (A) SSK, K16, SSK, K1. (58 sts)

Row 39: (A) P19, (B) P20, (A) P19.

Row 40: (A) K19, (B) K20, (A) K19.

Rows 41-47: Rpt last 2 rows 3 more times, then rpt Row 39 again.

Row 48: (A) K1, K2tog, K14, K2tog, (B) SSK, K16, K2tog, (A) SSK, K14, SSK, K1. (52 sts)

Row 49: (A) P17, (B) P18, (A) P17.

Row 50: (A) K17, (B) K18, (A) K17.

Rows 51-55: Rpt last 2 rows twice more, then rpt Row 49 again.

Row 56: (A) K1, K2tog, K12, K2tog, (B) SSK, K14, K2tog, (A) SSK, K12, SSK, K1. (46 sts)

Row 57: (A) P15, (B) P16, (A) P15.

Row 58: (A) K15, (B) K16, (A) K15.

Rows 59-61: Rpt last 2 rows once more, then rpt Row 57 again.

Row 62: (A) K1, K2tog, K10, K2tog, (B) SSK, K12, K2tog, (A) SSK, K10, SSK, K1. (40 sts)

Row 63: (A) P13, (B) P14, (A) P13.

Row 64: (A) K13, (B) K14, (A) K13.

Rows 65-67: Rpt last 2 rows once more, then rpt Row 63 again.

Row 68: (A) K1, K2tog, K8, K2tog, (B) SSK, K10, K2tog, (A) SSK, K8, SSK, K1. (34 sts)

Row 69: (A) P11, (B) P12, (A) P11.

Row 70: (A) K11, (B) K12, (A) K11.

Row 71: (A) P11, (B) P12, (A) P11.

Row 72: (A) K1, K2tog, K6, K2tog, (B) SSK, K8, K2tog, (A) SSK, K6, SSK, K1. (28 sts)

Row 73: (A) P9, (B) P10, (A) P9.

Row 74: (A) K9, (B) K10, (A) K9.

Row 75: (A) P9, (B) P10, (A) P9.

Row 76: (A) [K1, K2tog] 3 times, (B) [K1, K2tog] 3 times, K1, (A) [K2tog, K1] 3 times. (19 sts)

Row 77: (A) P6, (B) P7, (A) P6.

Continue in Yarn A only.

Row 78: K2tog to last st, K1. (10 sts)

Cut yarn leaving a long tail. Using a tapestry needle, thread tail through the stitches left on needle and pull up tight to gather stitches.

CONTRAST FRONT 2 (PHOTO 3)

Using Yarn A and 2.75mm straight needles, cast on 8 sts.

Rows 1-17: As Rows 1-17 of Standard Body – Plain.

Rows 18-23: Stocking stitch 6 rows.

Row 24: (A) K29, (C) K6, (A) K29.

Row 25: (A) P28, (C) P8, (A) P28.

Row 26: (A) K27, (C) K10, (A) K27.

Row 27: (A) P26, (C) P12, (A) P26.

Row 28: (A) K25, (C) K14, (A) K25.

Row 29: (A) P25, (C) P14, (A) P25.

Row 30: (A) K24, (C) K16, (A) K24.

Row 31: (A) P24, (C) P16, (A) P24.

Row 32: (A) K23, (C) K18, (A) K23.

Row 33: (A) P23, (C) P18, (A) P23.

Row 34: (A) K23, (C) K18, (A) K23.

Row 35: (A) P22, (C) P20, (A) P22.

Row 36: (A) K22, (C) K20, (A) K22.

Row 37: (A) P22, (C) P20, (A) P22.

Row 38: (A) K1, K2tog, K16, CDD, (C) K20, (A) CDD, K16, SSK, K1. (58 sts)

Row 39: (A) P19, (C) P20, (A) P19.

Row 40: (A) K19, (C) K20, (A) K19.

Rows 41-47: Rpt last 2 rows 3 more times, then rpt row 39 once more.

Row 48: (A) K1, K2tog, K14, K2tog, (C) SSK, K16, K2tog, (A) SSK, K14, SSK, K1. (52 sts)

Row 49: (A) P17, (C) P18, (A) P17.

Row 50: (A) K17, (C) K18, (A) K17.

Rows 51-55: Rpt last 2 rows 2 more times, then rpt row 49 once more.

Row 56: (A) K1, K2tog, K12, K2tog, (C) SSK, K14, K2tog, (A) SSK, K12, SSK, K1. (46 sts)

Row 57: (A) P15, (C) P16, (A) P15.

Row 58: (A) K15, (C) K16, (A) K15.

Rows 59-61: Rpt last 2 rows, then rpt row 57 once more.

Row 62: (A) K1, K2tog, K10, K2tog, (C) SSK, K12, K2tog, (A) SSK, K10, SSK, K1. (40 sts)

Row 63: (A) P13, (C) P14, (A) P13.

Row 64: (A) K13, (C) K14, (A) K13.

Rows 65-67: Rpt last 2 rows, then rpt row 63 once more.

Row 68: (A) K1, K2tog, K8, K2tog, (C) SSK, K10, K2tog, (A) SSK, K8, SSK, K1. (34 sts)

Row 69: (A) P11, (C) P12, (A) P11.

Row 70: (A) K11, (C) K12, (A) K11.

Row 71: (A) P11, (C) P12, (A) P11.

Row 72: (A) K1, K2tog, K6, K2tog, (C) SSK, K8, K2tog, (A) SSK, K6, SSK, K1. (28 sts)

Row 73: (A) P9, (C) P10, (A) P9.

Row 74: (A) K9, (C) K10, (A) K9.

Row 75: (A) P9, (C) P10, (A) P9.

Row 76: (A) [K1, K2tog] 3 times, (C) [K1, K2tog] 3 times, K1, (A) [K2tog, K1] 3 times. (19 sts)

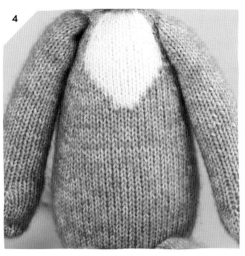
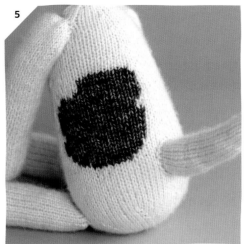

Row 77: (A) P6, (C) P7, (A) P6.

Continue in Yarn A only.

Row 78: K2tog to last st, K1. (10 sts)

Cut yarn leaving a long tail. Using a tapestry needle, thread tail through the stitches left on needle and pull up tight to gather stitches.

CHEST BLAZE (PHOTO 4)

Using Yarn A and 2.75mm straight needles, cast on 8 sts.

Rows 1-48: As Rows 1-48 of Standard Body – Plain.

Rows 49-51: Stocking stitch 3 rows.

Row 52: (A) K25, (B) K2, (A) K25.

Row 53: (A) P24, (B) P4, (A) P24.

Row 54: (A) K24, (B) K4, (A) K24.

Row 55: (A) P23, (B) P6, (A) P23.

Row 56: (A) K1, K2tog, K13, CDD, K4, (B) K6, (A) K4, CDD, K13, SSK, K1. (46 sts)

Row 57: (A) P19, (B) P8, (A) P19.

Row 58: (A) K19, (B) K8, (A) K19.

Row 59: (A) P18, (B) P10, (A) P18.

Row 60: (A) K18, (B) K10, (A) K18.

Row 61: (A) P17, (B) P12, (A) P17.

Row 62: (A) K1, K2tog, K11, CDD, (B) K12, (A) CDD, K11, SSK, K1. (40 sts)

Row 63: (A) P14, (B) P12, (A) P14.

Row 64: (A) K14, (B) K12, (A) K14.

Rows 65-67: Rpt last 2 rows once more, then rpt Row 63 again.

Row 68: (A) K1, K2tog, K9, K2tog, (B) SSK, K8, K2tog, (A) SSK, K9, SSK, K1. (34 sts)

Row 69: (A) P12, (B) P10, (A) P12.

Row 70: (A) K12, (B) K10, (A) K12.

Row 71: (A) P12, (B) P10, (A) P12.

Row 72: (A) K1, K2tog, K7, K2tog, (B) SSK, K6, K2tog, (A) SSK, K7, SSK, K1. (28 sts)

Row 73: (A) P10, (B) P8, (A) P10.

Row 74: (A) K10, (B) K8, (A) K10.

Row 75: (A) P10, (B) P8, (A) P10.

Row 76: (A) [K1, K2tog] 3 times, K1, (B) [K2tog, K1] twice, K2tog, (A) [K1, K2tog] 3 times, K1. (19 sts)

Row 77: (A) P7, (B) P5, (A) P7.

Continue in Yarn A only.

Row 78: K2tog to last st, K1. (10 sts)

Cut yarn leaving a long tail. Using a tapestry needle, thread tail through the stitches left on needle and pull up tight to gather stitches.

PATCH (PHOTO 5)

Using Yarn A and 2.75mm straight needles, cast on 8 sts.

Rows 1-29: As Rows 1-29 of Standard Body – Plain.

Row 30: (A) K7, (B) K7, (A) K50.

Row 31: (A) P48, (B) P10, (A) P6.

Row 32: (A) K5, (B) K12, (A) K47.

Row 33: (A) P46, (B) P13, (A) P5.

Row 34: (A) K5, (B) K13, (A) K46.

Row 35: (A) P45, (B) P15, (A) P4.

Row 36: (A) K4, (B) K15, (A) K45.

Row 37: (A) P45, (B) P15, (A) P4.

Row 38: (A) K1, K2tog, K1, (B) K15, (A) K1, CDD, K18, CDD, K17, SSK, K1. (58 sts)

Row 39: (A) P41, (B) P14, (A) P3.

Row 40: (A) K3, (B) K14, (A) K41.

Row 41: (A) P40, (B) P15, (A) P3.

Row 42: (A) K3, (B) K15, (A) K40.

Row 43: (A) P40, (B) P14, (A) P4.

Row 44: (A) K4, (B) K14, (A) K40.

Row 45: (A) P40, (B) P14, (A) P4.

Row 46: (A) K3, (B) K15, (A) K40.

Row 47: (A) P41, (B) P14, (A) P3.

Row 48: (A) K1, K2tog, (B) K14, (A) K1, CDD, K16, CDD, K15, SSK, K1. (52 sts)

Row 49: (A) P37, (B) P13, (A) P2.

Row 50: (A) K2, (B) K10, (A) K40.

Row 51: (A) P41, (B) P9, (A) P2.

Row 52: (A) K2, (B) K9, (A) K41.

Row 53: (A) P41, (B) P9, (A) P2.

Row 54: (A) K3, (B) K7, (A) K42.

Rows 55-78: As Rows 55-78 of Standard Body – Plain.

Cut yarn leaving a long tail. Using a tapestry needle, thread tail through the stitches left on needle and pull up tight to gather stitches.

ARMS (MAKE 2)

Using Yarn A and 2.75mm straight needles, cast on 14 sts.

Row 1 (ws): Purl.

Row 2: K1, [M1, K2] 6 times, M1, K1. (21 sts)

Rows 3-47: Stocking stitch 45 rows.

Row 48: K10, m1r, K1, m1l, K10. (23 sts)

Row 49: Purl.

Row 50: K11, m1r, K1, m1l, K11. (25 sts)

Rows 51-55: Stocking stitch 5 rows.

Row 56: K7, K2tog twice, CDD, SSK twice, K7. (19 sts)

Rows 57-61: Stocking stitch 5 rows.

Row 62: K1, K2tog 4 times, K1, SSK 4 times, K1. (11 sts)

Row 63: Purl.

Cut yarn leaving a long tail. Using a tapestry needle, thread tail through the stitches left on needle and pull up tight to gather stitches.

CONTRAST PAW (PHOTO 6)

LEFT ARM

Using Yarn A and 2.75mm straight needles, cast on 14 sts.

Row 1 (ws): Purl.

Row 2: K1, [M1, K2] 6 times, M1, K1. (21 sts)

Rows 3-41: Stocking stitch 39 rows.

Row 42: (A) K4, (B) K4, (A) K13.

Row 43: (A) P12, (B) P6, (A) P3.

Row 44: (A) K3, (B) K6, (A) K12.

Row 45: (A) P11, (B) P8, (A) P2.

Row 46: (A) K2, (B) K8, (A) K11.

Row 47: (A) P11, (B) P8, (A) P2.

Row 48: (A) K1, (B) K8, m1r, K1, (A) K1, m1l, K10. (23 sts)

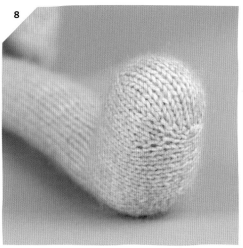

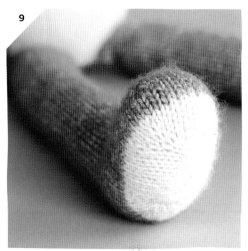

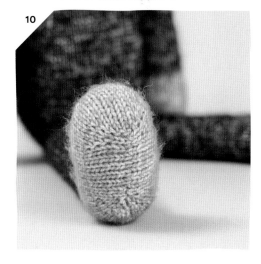

Row 49: (A) P12, (B) P10, (A) P1.

Row 50: (A) K1, (B) K9, m1r, K1, (A) K1, m1l, K11. (25 sts)

Row 51: (A) P13, (B) P11, (A) P1.

Row 52: (A) K1, (B) K11, (A) K13.

Rows 53-54: Rpt last 2 rows once more.

Row 55: (A) P10, SSP, P1, (B) P2tog, P9, (A) P1. (23 sts)

Row 56: (A) K1, (B) K6, K2tog twice, (A) K1, SSK twice, K7. (19 sts)

Row 57: (A) P10, (B) P8, (A) P1.

Row 58: (A) K1, (B) K8, (A) K10.

Rows 59-61: Rpt rows 57-58, then work row

57 once more.

Row 62: (A) K1, (B) K2tog 4 times, (A) K1, SSK 4

times, K1. (11 sts)

Continue in Yarn A only.

Row 63: Purl.

Cut yarn leaving a long tail. Using a tapestry

needle, thread tail through the stitches left

on needle and pull up tight to gather stitches.

RIGHT ARM

Using Yarn A and 2.75mm straight needles, cast on 14 sts.

Row 1 (ws): Purl.

Row 2: K1, [M1, K2] 6 times, M1, K1. (21 sts)

Rows 3-41: Stocking stitch 39 rows.

Row 42: (A) K13, (B) K4, (A) K4.

Row 43: (A) P3, (B) P6, (A) P12.

Row 44: (A) K12, (B) K6, (A) K3.

Row 45: (A) P2, (B) P8, (A) P11.

Row 46: (A) K11, (B) K8, (A) K2.

Row 47: (A) P2, (B) P8, (A) P11.

Row 48: (A) K10, m1r, K1, (B) K1, m1l, K8, (A) K1. (23 sts)

Row 49: (A) P1, (B) P10, (A) P12.

Row 50: (A) K11, m1r, K1, (B) K1, m1l, K9, (A) K1. (25 sts)

Row 51: (A) P1, (B) P11, (A) P13.

Row 52: (A) K13, (B) K11, (A) K1.

Rows 53-54: Rpt last 2 rows once more.

Row 55: (A) P1, (B) P9, SSP, (A) P1, P2tog, P10. (23 sts)

Row 56: (A) K7, K2tog twice, K1, (B) SSK twice, K6, (A) K1. (19 sts)

Row 57: (A) P1, (B) P8, (A) P10.

Row 58: (A) K10, (B) K8, (A) K1.

Rows 59-61: Rpt rows 57-58, then work row 57 once more.

Row 62: (A) K1, K2tog 4 times, K1, (B) SSK 4 times (A) K1. (11 sts)

Continue in Yarn A only.

Row 63: Purl.

Cut yarn leaving a long tail. Using a tapestry needle, thread tail through the stitches left on needle and pull up tight to gather stitches.

CONTRAST HAND (PHOTO 7)

As Standard Arms – Plain, but cast on and work Rows 1-43 using Yarn A, then work remainder using Yarn B.

LEGS (MAKE 2)

PLAIN (PHOTO 8)

Using Yarn A and 2.75mm straight needles, cast on 20 sts.

Row 1 (ws): Purl.

Row 2: K1, M1, K6, [K2, M1] twice, K8, M1, K1. (24 sts)

Row 3: Purl.

Row 4: [K1, M1] twice, K6, [K1, M1] twice, K3, [K1, M1] twice, K6, [K1, M1] twice, K1. (32 sts)

Row 5: Purl.

Row 6: [K2, M1] twice, K5, [K2, M1] twice, K4, [K2, M1] twice, K5, [K2, M1] twice, K2. (40 sts)

Row 7: Purl.

Row 8: [K3, M1] twice, K4, [K3, M1] twice, K5, [K3, M1] twice, K4, [K3, M1] twice, K3. (48 sts)

Rows 9-13: Stocking stitch 5 rows.

Row 14: K19, SSK, K6, K2tog, K19. (46 sts)

Row 15: Purl.

Row 16: K19, SSK, K4, K2tog, K19. (44 sts)

Row 17: Purl.

Row 18: K19, SSK, K2, K2tog, K19. (42 sts)

Row 19: Purl.

Row 20: K11, [K8, SSK, K2tog, K8] and cast off these 18 sts as you work them, K to end. (22 sts)

Row 21: P10, P2tog, P10. (21 sts)

Rows 22-89: Stocking stitch 68 rows.

Cast off.

CONTRAST FOOT PAD (PHOTO 9)

As Standard Legs – Plain, but cast on and work Rows 1-8 using Yarn B, then work remainder using Yarn A.

CONTRAST FOOT (PHOTO 10)

As Standard Legs – Plain, but cast on and work Rows 1-20 using Yarn B, then work remainder using Yarn A.

George

THE DOG

• •

YOU WILL NEED

- Scheepjes Stonewashed (50g/130m; 78% cotton/22% acrylic) yarn in the following shades:

  - *Yarn A* Cream (Moonstone 801), 2 balls

  - *Yarn B* Black (Black Onyx 803), 1 ball

- 2.75mm (US 2) straight needles

- Toy stuffing

- 2 x 10mm (½in) buttons

- Scrap piece of 4-ply yarn for embroidering nose

Before you start, please read the Essential Notes at the beginning of this book.

DOG PATTERN

HEAD

Starting at neck:

Using Yarn A and 2.75mm straight needles, cast on 11 sts.

Row 1 (ws): Purl.

Row 2: [K1, M1] to last st, K1. (21 sts)

Row 3: Purl.

Row 4: [K2, M1] to last st, K1. (31 sts)

Row 5: Purl.

Row 6: [K1, m1l, K14, m1r] twice, K1. (35 sts)

Row 7: Purl.

Row 8: [K1, m1l, K16, m1r] twice, K1. (39 sts)

Row 9: P19, m1pl, P1, m1pr, P19. (41 sts)

Row 10: [K1, m1l, K19, m1r] twice, K1. (45 sts)

Row 11: P22, m1pl, P1, m1pr, P22. (47 sts)

Row 12: [K1, m1l, K22, m1r] twice, K1. (51 sts)

Row 13: P25, m1pl, P1, m1pr, P25. (53 sts)

Row 14: K26, m1r, K1, m1l, K26. (55 sts)

Row 15: Purl.

Row 16: [K1, m1l, K26, m1r] twice, K1. (59 sts)

Row 17: Purl.

Row 18: (A) K29, sl1, K12, (B) K6, (A) K11.

Row 19: (A) P10, (B) P9, (A) P40.

Row 20: (A) K29, sl1, K9, (B) K11, (A) K9.

Row 21: (A) P9, (B) P11, (A) P39.

Row 22: (A) K29, sl1, K8, (B) K13, (A) K8.

Row 23: (A) P8, (B) P13, (A) P7, PCDD, P28. (57 sts)

Row 24: (A) K27, CDD, K6, (B) K14, (A) K7. (55 sts)

Row 25: (A) P7, (B) P14, (A) P5, PCDD, P26. (53 sts)

Row 26: (A) K25, CDD, K4, (B) K14, (A) K7. (51 sts)

Row 27: (A) P7, (B) P14, (A) P3, PCDD, P24. (49 sts)

Row 28: (A) K1, K2tog, K20, CDD, K3, (B) K13, (A) K4, SSK, K1. (45 sts)

Row 29: (A) P6, (B) P13, (A) P2, PCDD, P21. (43 sts)

Row 30: (A) K20, CDD, K1, (B) K13, (A) K6. (41 sts)

Row 31: (A) P6, (B) P12, (A) P23.

Row 32: (A) K1, K2tog, K17, sl1, K2, (B) K12, (A) K3, SSK, K1. (39 sts)

Row 33: (A) P5, (B) P12, (A) P22.

Row 34: (A) K19, sl1, K3, (B) K11, (A) K5.

Row 35: (A) P5, (B) P11, (A) P23.

Row 36: (A) K1, K2tog, K16, sl1, K3, (B) K11, (A) K2, SSK, K1. (37 sts)

Row 37: (A) P4, (B) P10, (A) P23.

Row 38: (A) K18, sl1, K5, (B) K8, (A) K5.

Continue in Yarn A only.

Row 39: Purl.

Row 40: K1, K2tog, K3, K2tog 4 times, K3, CDD, K3, SSK 4 times, K3, SSK, K1. (25 sts)

Row 41: Purl.

Row 42: K1, K2tog 5 times, CDD, SSK 5 times, K1. (13 sts)

Row 43: Purl.

Cast off.

EARS (MAKE 2)

Using Yarn B and 2.75mm straight needles, cast on 31 sts.

Row 1 (ws): Purl.

Rows 2-7: Stocking stitch 6 rows.

Row 8: [K6, K2tog, SSK, K5] twice, K1. (27 sts)

Rows 9-11: Stocking stitch 3 rows.

Row 12: [K5, K2tog, SSK, K4] twice, K1. (23 sts)

Rows 13-15: Stocking stitch 3 rows.

Row 16: [K4, K2tog, SSK, K3] twice, K1. (19 sts)

Rows 17-19: Stocking stitch 3 rows.

Row 20: [K3, K2tog, SSK, K2] twice, K1. (15 sts)

Rows 21-23: Stocking stitch 3 rows.

Row 24: [K2, K2tog, SSK, K1] twice, K1. (11 sts)

Row 25: Purl.

Row 26: [K1, K2tog, SSK] twice, K1. (7 sts)

Cut yarn leaving a long tail. Using a tapestry needle, thread tail through the stitches left on needle and pull up tight to gather stitches.

TAIL

Using Yarn A and 2.75mm straight needles, cast on 18 sts.

Row 1 (ws): Purl.

Rows 2-7: Stocking stitch 6 rows.

Row 8: K1, K2tog, K12, SSK, K1. (16 sts)

Rows 9-15: Stocking stitch 7 rows.

Row 16: K1, K2tog, K10, SSK, K1. (14 sts)

Rows 17-31: Stocking stitch 15 rows.

Row 32: K1, K2tog, K8, SSK, K1. (12 sts)

Rows 33-37: Stocking stitch 5 rows.

Row 38: K1, K2tog, K6, SSK, K1. (10 sts)

Rows 39-41: Stocking stitch 3 rows.

Row 42: K1, K2tog, K4, SSK, K1. (8 sts)

Row 43: Purl.

Row 44: K1, K2tog twice, SSK, K1. (5 sts)

Row 45: Purl.

Cut yarn leaving a long tail. Using a tapestry needle, thread tail through the stitches left on needle and pull up tight to gather stitches.

BODY

Work as Standard Body – Patch (see Standard Body Parts).

ARMS (MAKE 2)

Work as Standard Arms (see Standard Body Parts).

LEGS (MAKE 2)

Work as Standard Legs – Contrast Foot Pad (see Standard Body Parts).

MAKING UP

Follow the instructions in the techniques section (see Techniques: Making Up Your Animal).

Bella

THE CAT

· · · · ● ● ● ● ● ● ● ● ● ● ● ● · ·

YOU WILL NEED

- Scheepjes Stonewashed (50g/130m;
  78% cotton/22% acrylic) yarn
  in the following shades:

  - **Yarn A** *Mustard (Yellow Jasper 809), 2 balls*

  - **Yarn B** *Cream (Moonstone 801), 1 ball*

- 2.75mm (US 2) straight needles

- Toy stuffing

- 2 x 10mm (½in) buttons

- Scrap piece of 4-ply yarn for
  embroidering nose

*Before you start, please read the Essential Notes
at the beginning of this book.*

CAT PATTERN

HEAD

Starting at neck:

Using 2.75mm straight needles and Yarn A, cast on 11 sts.

Row 1 (ws): Purl.

Row 2: [K1, M1] to last st, K1. (21 sts)

Row 3: Purl.

Row 4: [K2, M1] to last st, K1. (31 sts)

Row 5: Purl.

Row 6: K1, m1l, knit to last st, m1r, K1. (33 sts)

Row 7: Purl.

Row 8: [K1, m1l, K15, m1r] twice, K1. (37 sts)

Row 9: P18, m1pl, P1, m1pr, P18. (39 sts)

Row 10: (A) K1, m1l, K16, (B) [m1l, K1] twice, m1l, (A) K1, (B) [m1r, K1] twice, m1r, (A) K16, m1r, K1. (47 sts)

Row 11: (A) P18, (B) P1, m1pr, P4, (A) K1, (B) P4, m1pl, P1, (A) P18. (49 sts)

Row 12: (A) K1, m1l, K17, (B) K1, m1l, K11, m1r, K1, (A) K17, m1r, K1. (53 sts)

Row 13: (A) P19, (B) P1, m1pr, P13, m1pl, P1, (A) P19. (55 sts)

Row 14: (A) K19, (B) K1, m1l, K15, m1r, K1, (A) K19. (57 sts)

Row 15: (A) P19, (B) P19, (A) P19.

Row 16: (A) K1, m1l, K18, (B) K19, (A) K18, m1r, K1. (59 sts)

Row 17: (A) P20, (B) P19, (A) P20.

Row 18: (A) K20, (B) K19, (A) K20.

Row 19: (A) P20, (B) P3tog, P13, SSSP, (A) P20. (55 sts)

Row 20: (A) K20, (B) SSSK, K9, K3tog, (A) K20. (51 sts)

Row 21: (A) P20, (B) P3tog, P5, SSSP, (A) P20. (47 sts)

Row 22: (A) K20, (B) SSSK, K1, K3tog, (A) K20. (43 sts)

Row 23: (A) P20, (B) P3, (A) P20.

Row 24: (A) K20, (B) K3, (A) K20.

Row 25: (A) P20, (B) P3, (A) P20.

Continue in Yarn A only.

Row 26: K21, sl1, K21.

Row 27: Purl.

Row 28: K1, K2tog, K18, sl1, K18, SSK, K1. (41 sts)

Row 29: Purl.

Row 30: K20, sl1, K20.

Row 31: Purl.

Row 32: K1, K2tog, K17, sl1, K17, SSK, K1. (39 sts)

Row 33: Purl.

Row 34: K19, sl1, K19.

Row 35: Purl.

Row 36: K1, K2tog, K16, sl1, K16, SSK, K1. (37 sts)

Row 37: Purl.

Row 38: K18, sl1, K18.

Row 39: Purl.

Row 40: K1, K2tog, K3, K2tog 4 times, K3, CDD, K3, SSK 4 times, K3, SSK, K1. (25 sts)

Row 41: Purl.

Row 42: K1, K2tog 5 times, CDD, SSK 5 times, K1. (13 sts)

Row 43: Purl.

Cast off.

EARS (MAKE 2)

Using 2.75mm straight needles and Yarn A, cast on 21 sts.

Row 1 (ws): (A) P8, (B) P5, (A) P8.

Row 2: (A) K8, (B) [K1, M1] 4 times, K1, (A) K8. (25 sts)

Row 3: (A) P8, (B) P9, (A) P8.

Row 4: (A) K5, K2tog, K1, (B) SSK, K5, K2tog, (A) K1, SSK, K5. (21 sts)

Row 5: (A) P7, (B) P7, (A) P7.

Row 6: (A) K4, K2tog, K1, (B) SSK, K3, K2tog, (A) K1, SSK, K4. (17 sts)

Row 7: (A) P6, (B) P5, (A) P6.

Row 8: (A) K3, K2tog, K1, (B) SSK, K1, K2tog, (A) K1, SSK, K3. (13 sts)

Row 9: (A) P5, (B) P3, (A) P5.

Row 10: (A) K2, K2tog, SSK, (B) K1, (A) K2tog, SSK, K2. (9 sts)

Continue in Yarn A only.

Row 11: Purl.

Row 12: K1, K2tog, sl1 kw, K2tog, PSSO, SSK, K1. (5 sts)

Cut yarn leaving a long tail. Using a tapestry needle, thread tail through the stitches left on needle and pull up tight to gather stitches.

TAIL

Using 2.75mm straight needles and Yarn A, cast on 12 sts.

Row 1 (ws): Purl.

Rows 2–79: Stocking stitch 78 rows.

Change to Yarn B.

Rows 80–86: Stocking stitch 7 rows.

Cut yarn leaving a long tail. Using a tapestry needle, thread tail through the stitches left on needle and pull up tight to gather stitches.

BODY

Work as Standard Body – Chest Blaze (see Standard Body Parts).

ARMS (MAKE 2)

Work as Standard Arms (see Standard Body Parts).

LEGS (MAKE 2)

Work as Standard Legs – Contrast Foot Pad (see Standard Body Parts).

MAKING UP

Follow the instructions in the techniques section (see Techniques: Making Up Your Animal).

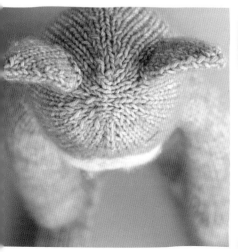

Noah
THE HORSE

YOU WILL NEED

- Scheepjes Stonewashed (50g/130m; 78% cotton/22% acrylic) yarn in the following shades:

  - *Yarn A* Brown (Boulder Opal 804), 2 balls

  - *Yarn B* Cream (Moonstone 801), 1 ball

- 2.75mm (US 2) straight needles

- Toy stuffing

- 2 x 10mm (½in) buttons

- Scrap piece of 4-ply yarn for embroidering nostrils

Before you start, please read the Essential Notes at the beginning of this book.

HORSE PATTERN

HEAD

Starting at neck:

Using Yarn A and 2.75mm straight needles, cast on 11 sts.

Row 1 (ws): Purl.

Row 2: [K1, M1] to last st, K1. (21 sts)

Row 3: Purl.

Row 4: [K2, M1] to last st, K1. (31 sts)

Row 5: Purl.

Row 6: K1, m1l, K13, m1r, K3, m1l, K13, m1r, K1. (35 sts)

Row 7: Purl.

Row 8: K1, m1l, K15, m1r, K3, m1l, K15, m1r, K1. (39 sts)

Row 9: P18, m1pl, P3, m1pr, P18. (41 sts)

Row 10: K1, m1l, K18, m1r, K3, m1l, K18, m1r, K1. (45 sts)

Row 11: P21, m1pl, P3, m1pr, P21. (47 sts)

Row 12: K1, m1l, K21, m1r, K3, m1l, K21, m1r, K1. (51 sts)

Row 13: P24, m1pl, P3, m1pr, P24. (53 sts)

Row 14: K25, m1r, K3, m1l, K25. (55 sts)

Row 15: (A) P25, (B) [m1pr, P1] 3 times, [m1pl, P1] twice, m1pl, (A) P25. (61 sts)

Row 16: (A) K1, m1l, K24, (B) K1, m1l, K9, m1r, K1, (A) K24, m1r, K1. (65 sts)

Row 17: (A) P26, (B) P1, m1pr, P11, m1pl, P1, (A) P26. (67 sts)

Row 18: (A) K26, (B) K1, m1l, K13, m1r, K1, (A) K26. (69 sts)

Row 19: (A) P26, (B) P1, m1pr, P15, m1pl, P1, (A) P26. (71 sts)

Row 20: (A) K26, (B) K1, m1l, K17, m1r, K1, (A) K26. (73 sts)

Row 21: (A) P26, (B) P21, (A) P26.

Row 22: (A) K26, (B) K21, (A) K26.

Rows 23–25: Rpt last 2 rows once more, then rpt Row 21 again.

Row 26: (A) K26, (B) SSK, K17, K2tog, (A) K26. (71 sts)

Row 27: (A) P26, (B) P3tog, P13, SSSP, (A) P26. (67 sts)

Row 28: (A) K1, K2tog, K23, (B) SSSK, K9, K3tog, (A) K23, SSK, K1. (61 sts)

Row 29: (A) P25, (B) P3tog, P5, SSSP, (A) P25. (57 sts)

Row 30: (A) K25, (B) SSSK, K1, K3tog, (A) K25. (53 sts)

Row 31: (A) P23, SSP, (B) P3, (A) P2tog, P23. (51 sts)

Row 32: (A) K1, K2tog, K19, K2tog, (B) K3, (A) SSK, K19, SSK, K1. (47 sts)

Row 33: (A) P20, SSP, (B) P3, (A) P2tog, P20. (45 sts)

Row 34: (A) K19, K2tog, (B) K3, (A) SSK, K19. (43 sts)

Row 35: (A) P18, SSP, (B) P3, (A) P2tog, P18. (41 sts)

Row 36: (A) K1, K2tog, K14, K2tog, (B) K3, (A) SSK, K14, SSK, K1. (37 sts)

Row 37: (A) P17, (B) P3, (A) P17.

Row 38: (A) K17, (B) K3, (A) K17.

Row 39: (A) P17, (B) P3, (A) P17.

Row 40: (A) K1, K2tog, K3, K2tog 4 times, K3, (B) K3, (A) K3, SSK 4 times, K3, SSK, K1. (27 sts)

Row 41: (A) P12, (B) P3, (A) P12.

Continue in Yarn A only.

Row 42: K1, K2tog 5 times, K1, sl1 kw, K2tog, PSSO, K1, SSK 5 times, K1. (15 sts)

Row 43: Purl.

Cast off.

EARS (MAKE 2)

Using Yarn A and 2.75mm straight needles, cast on 14 sts.

Row 1 (ws): Purl.

Row 2: K5, [K1, M1] 3 times, knit to end. (17 sts)

Rows 3-9: Stocking stitch 7 rows.

Row 10: [K3, K2tog, SSK] twice, K3. (13 sts)

Row 11: Purl.

Row 12: K1, [K1, K2tog, SSK] twice, K2. (9 sts)

Row 13: Purl.

Row 14: K1, K2tog, sl1 kw, K2tog, PSSO, SSK, K1. (5 sts)

Row 15: Purl.

Row 16: Knit.

Cut yarn leaving a long tail. Using a tapestry needle, thread tail through the stitches left on needle and pull up tight to gather stitches.

MANE

Using Yarn B and 2.75mm dpns, cast on 4 sts for each i-cord (see Techniques: Casting On and Stitches, Making i-cord).

Make 14 i-cords, 8 rows long.

TAIL

Using Yarn B and 2.75mm dpns, cast on 4 sts for each i-cord (see Techniques: Casting On and Stitches, Making i-cord).

Make 2 i-cords 45 rows long.

Make 1 i-cord 40 rows long.

Make 1 i-cord 35 rows long

Make 1 i-cord 30 rows long.

BODY

Work as Standard Body – Plain (see Standard Body Parts).

ARMS (MAKE 2)

Work as Standard Arms (see Standard Body Parts).

LEGS (MAKE 2)

Work as Standard Legs – Plain (see Standard Body Parts).

MAKING UP

Follow the instructions in the techniques section (see Techniques: Making Up Your Animal).

Dorothy
THE MOUSE

● ● ● ● ● ● ● ● ● ● ● ● ● ● ●

YOU WILL NEED

- Scheepjes Stonewashed (50g/130m;
  78% cotton/22% acrylic) yarn
  in the following shade:

  - **Yarn A** *Pale Grey (Crystal Quartz 814), 2 balls*

- 2.75mm (US 2) straight needles

- Toy stuffing

- 2 x 10mm (½in) buttons

- Scrap piece of 4-ply yarn for
  embroidering nose

*Before you start, please read the Essential Notes
at the beginning of this book.*

MOUSE PATTERN

HEAD

Starting at neck:

Using Yarn A and 2.75mm straight needles, cast on 11 sts.

Row 1 (ws): Purl.

Row 2: [K1, M1] to last st, K1. (21 sts)

Row 3: Purl.

Row 4: [K2, M1] to last st, K1. (31 sts)

Row 5: Purl.

Row 6: [K1, m1l, K14, m1r] twice, K1. (35 sts)

Row 7: Purl.

Row 8: [K1, m1l, K16, m1r] twice, K1. (39 sts)

Row 9: P19, m1pl, P1, m1pr, P19. (41 sts)

Row 10: [K1, m1l, K19, m1r] twice, K1. (45 sts)

Row 11: P22, m1pl, P1, m1pr, P22. (47 sts)

Row 12: [K1, m1l, K22, m1r] twice, K1. (51 sts)

Row 13: P25, m1pl, P1, m1pr, P25. (53 sts)

Row 14: K26, m1r, K1, m1l, K26. (55 sts)

Row 15: Purl.

Row 16: [K1, m1l, K26, m1r] twice, K1. (59 sts)

Row 17: Purl.

Row 18: K29, sl1, K29.

Row 19: Purl.

Row 20: K28, CDD, K28. (57 sts)

Row 21: Purl.

Row 22: K27, CDD, K27. (55 sts)

Row 23: Purl.

Row 24: K26, CDD, K26. (53 sts)

Row 25: Purl.

Row 26: K25, CDD, K25. (51 sts)

Row 27: Purl.

Row 28: K1, K2tog, K21, CDD, K21, SSK, K1. (47 sts)

Row 29: Purl.

Row 30: K22, CDD, K22. (45 sts)

Row 31: Purl.

Row 32: K1, K2tog, K18, CDD, K18, SSK, K1. (41 sts)

Row 33: Purl.

Row 34: K19, CDD, K19. (39 sts)

Row 35: Purl.

Row 36: K1, K2tog, K16, sl1, K16, SSK, K1. (37 sts)

Row 37: Purl.

Row 38: K18, sl1, K18.

Row 39: Purl.

Row 40: K1, K2tog, K3, K2tog 4 times, K3, CDD, K3, SSK 4 times, K3, SSK, K1. (25 sts)

Row 41: Purl.

Row 42: K1, K2tog 5 times, CDD, SSK 5 times, K1. (13 sts)

Row 43: Purl.

Cast off.

EARS (MAKE 2)

Using Yarn A and 2.75mm straight needles, cast on 25 sts.

Row 1 (ws): Purl.

Row 2: K7, M1, K2, [M1, K1] 8 times, K1, M1, K7. (35 sts)

Rows 3-7: Stocking stitch 5 rows.

Row 8: [K7, K2tog, SSK, K6] twice, K1. (31 sts)

Rows 9-11: Stocking stitch 3 rows.

Row 12: [K6, K2tog, SSK, K5] twice, K1. (27 sts)

Row 13: Purl.

Row 14: [K5, K2tog, SSK, K4] twice, K1. (23 sts)

Row 15: Purl.

Row 16: [K4, K2tog, SSK, K3] twice, K1. (19 sts)

Row 17: [P3, SSP, P2tog, P2] twice, P1. (15 sts)

Cut yarn leaving a long tail. Using a tapestry needle, thread tail through the stitches left on needle and pull up tight to gather stitches.

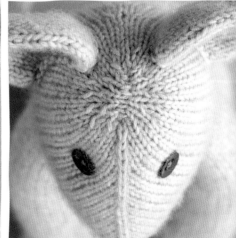

TAIL

Using Yarn A and 2.75mm straight needles, cast on 16 sts.

Row 1 (ws): Purl.

Rows 2-7: Stocking stitch 6 rows.

Row 8: [K1, K2tog, K2, SSK, K1] twice. (12 sts)

Rows 9-15: Stocking stitch 7 rows.

Row 16: [K1, K2tog, K1, SSK] twice. (8 sts)

Rows 17-77: Stocking stitch 61 rows.

Row 78: K1, K2tog 3 times, K1. (5 sts)

Row 79: Purl.

Cut yarn leaving a long tail. Using a tapestry needle, thread tail through the stitches left on needle and pull up tight to gather stitches.

BODY

Work as Standard Body – Plain (see Standard Body Parts).

ARMS (MAKE 2)

Work as Standard Arms (see Standard Body Parts).

LEGS (MAKE 2)

Work as Standard Legs – Plain (see Standard Body Parts).

MAKING UP

Follow the instructions in the techniques section (see Techniques: Making Up Your Animal).

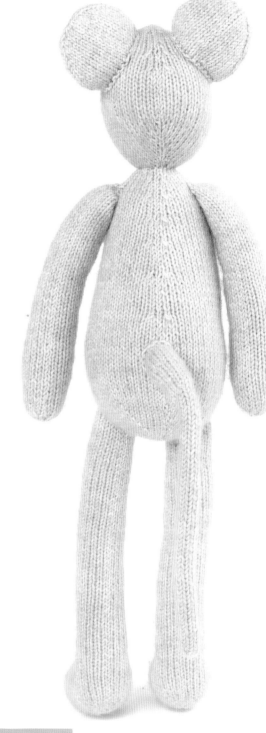

Charlotte

THE FOX

• • • • • • • • • • • • • • • • •

YOU WILL NEED

- Scheepjes Stonewashed (50g/130m;
  78% cotton/ 22% acrylic) yarn
  in the following shades:

  - **Yarn A** *Orange (Coral 816), 2 balls*

  - **Yarn B** *Cream (Moonstone 801), 1 ball*

- 2.75mm (US 2) straight needles

- Toy stuffing

- 2 x 10mm (½in) buttons

- Scrap piece of 4-ply yarn for
  embroidering nose

*Before you start, please read the Essential Notes
at the beginning of this book.*

FOX PATTERN

HEAD

Starting at neck:

Using Yarn A and 2.75mm straight needles, cast on 11 sts.

Row 1 (ws): (A) P4, (B) P3, (A) P4.

Row 2: (A) [K1, M1] 3 times, K1, (B) [M1, K1] 3 times, M1, (A) [K1, M1] 3 times, K1. (21 sts)

Row 3: (A) P7, (B) P7, (A) P7.

Row 4: (A) [K2, M1] 3 times, K1, (B) K1, M1, [K2, M1] 3 times, (A) [K2, M1] 3 times, K1. (31 sts)

Row 5: (A) P10, (B) P11, (A) P10.

Row 6: (A) K1, m1l, K9, (B) K11, (A) K9, m1r, K1. (33 sts)

Row 7: (A) P11, (B) P11, (A) P11.

Row 8: (A) K1, m1l, K10, (B) K5, m1r, K1, m1l, K5, (A) K10, m1r, K1. (37 sts)

Row 9: (A) P12, (B) P13, (A) P12.

Row 10: (A) K1, m1l, K11, (B) K6, m1r, K1, m1l, K6, (A) K11, m1r, K1. (41 sts)

Row 11: (A) P13, (B) P7, m1pl, P1, m1pr, P7, (A) P13. (43 sts)

Row 12: (A) K1, m1l, K12, (B) K8, m1r, K1, m1l, K8, (A) K12, m1r, K1. (47 sts)

Row 13: (A) P14, (B) P9, m1pl, P1, m1pr, P9, (A) P14. (49 sts)

Row 14: (A) K14, (B) K10, m1r, K1, m1l, K10, (A) K14. (51 sts)

Row 15: (A) P14, (B) P11, m1pl, P1, m1pr, P11, (A) P14. (53 sts)

Row 16: (A) K1, m1l, K13, (B) K12, m1r, K1, m1l, K12, (A) K13, m1r, K1. (57 sts)

Row 17: (A) P15, (B) P27, (A) P15.

Row 18: (A) K15, (B) K13, m1r, K1, m1l, K13, (A) K15. (59 sts)

Row 19: (A) P15, (B) P29, (A) P15.

Row 20: (A) K16, (B) K13, sl1, K13, (A) K16.

Row 21: (A) P16, (B) P27, (A) P16.

Row 22: (A) K17, (B) K11, CDD, K11, (A) K17. (57 sts)

Continue in Yarn A only.

Row 23: Purl.

Row 24: K27, CDD, K27. (55 sts)

Row 25: P26, PCDD, P26. (53 sts)

Row 26: K25, CDD, K25. (51 sts)

Row 27: P24, PCDD, P24. (49 sts)

Row 28: K1, K2tog, K20, CDD, K20, SSK, K1. (45 sts)

Row 29: P21, PCDD, P21. (43 sts)

Row 30: K20, CDD, K20. (41 sts)

Row 31: Purl.

Row 32: K1, K2tog, K17, sl1, K17, SSK, K1. (39 sts)

Row 33: Purl.

Row 34: K19, sl1, K19.

Row 35: Purl.

Row 36: K1, K2tog, K16, sl1, K16, SSK, K1. (37 sts)

Row 37: Purl.

Row 38: K18, sl1, K18.

Row 39: Purl.

Row 40: K1, K2tog, K3, K2tog 4 times, K3, CDD, K3, SSK 4 times, K3, SSK, K1. (25 sts)

Row 41: Purl.

Row 42: K1, K2tog 5 times, CDD, SSK 5 times, K1. (13 sts)

Row 43: Purl.

Cast off.

EARS (MAKE 2)

Using Yarn A and 2.75mm straight needles, cast on 21 sts.

Row 1 (ws): (A) P8, (B) P5, (A) P8.

Row 2: (A) K8, (B) [K1, M1] 4 times, K1, (A) K8. (25 sts)

Row 3: (A) P8, (B) P9, (A) P8.

Row 4: (A) K8, (B) K9, (A) K8.

Rows 5-7: Rpt last 2 rows once more, then rpt Row 3 again.

Row 8: (A) K5, K2tog, K1, (B) SSK, K5, K2tog, (A) K1, SSK, K5. (21 sts)

Row 9: (A) P7, (B) P7, (A) P7.

Row 10: (A) K7, (B) K7, (A) K7.

Row 11: (A) P7, (B) P7, (A) P7.

Row 12: (A) K4, K2tog, K1, (B) SSK, K3, K2tog, (A) K1, SSK, K4. (17 sts)

Row 13: (A) P6, (B) P5, (A) P6.

Row 14: (A) K3, K2tog, K1, (B) SSK, K1, K2tog, (A) K1, SSK, K3. (13 sts)

Row 15: (A) P5, (B) P3, (A) P5.

Continue in Yarn A only.

Row 16: K2, K2tog, SSK, K1, K2tog, SSK, K2. (9 sts)

Row 17: Purl.

Row 18: K1, K2tog, sl1 kw, K2tog, PSSO, SSK, K1. (5 sts)

Row 19: Purl.

Cut yarn leaving a long tail. Using a tapestry needle, thread tail through the stitches left on needle and pull up tight to gather stitches.

TAIL

Using Yarn A and 2.75mm straight needles, cast on 19 sts.

Row 1 (ws): Purl.

Rows 2-5: Stocking stitch 4 rows.

Row 6: K4, [M1, K6] twice, M1, K3. (22 sts)

Rows 7-9: Stocking stitch 3 rows.

Row 10: K1, [M1, K7] 3 times. (25 sts)

Rows 11-13: Stocking stitch 3 rows.

Row 14: K3, [M1, K4] 5 times, M1, K2. (31 sts)

Rows 15-36: Stocking stitch 22 rows.

Change to Yarn B.

Row 37: Purl.

Row 38: K6, SSK, K1, K2tog, K20. (29 sts)

Row 39: Purl.

Row 40: K19, SSK, K1, K2tog, K5. (27 sts)

Row 41: Purl.

Row 42: K5, SSK, K1, K2tog, K17. (25 sts)

Row 43: Purl.

Row 44: [K4, SSK, K1, K2tog, K3] twice, K1. (21 sts)

Row 45: Purl.

Row 46: [K3, SSK, K1, K2tog, K2] twice, K1. (17 sts)

Row 47: Purl.

Row 48: [K2, SSK, K1, K2tog, K1] twice, K1. (13 sts)

Row 49: Purl.

Row 50: [K1, SSK, K1, K2tog] twice, K1. (9 sts)

Row 51: Purl.

Row 52: SSK, K1, K2tog, CDD, K1. (5 sts)

Rows 53-54: Stocking stitch 2 rows.

Cut yarn leaving a long tail. Using a tapestry needle, thread tail through the stitches left on needle and pull up tight to gather stitches.

BODY

Work as Standard Body – Contrast Front 1 (see Standard Body Parts).

ARMS (MAKE 2)

Work as Standard Arms (see Standard Body Parts).

LEGS (MAKE 2)

Work as Standard Legs – Contrast Foot Pad (see Standard Body Parts).

MAKING UP

Follow the instructions in the techniques section (see Techniques: Making Up Your Animal).

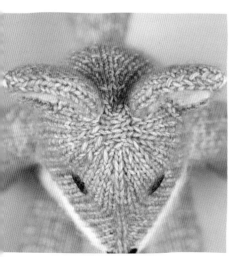

Archie

THE SQUIRREL

YOU WILL NEED

- Scheepjes Stonewashed (50g/130m; 78% cotton/22% acrylic) yarn in the following shades:

  - *Yarn A* Orange (Coral 816), 2 balls

  - *Yarn B* Cream (Moonstone 801), 1 ball

- 2.75mm (US 2) straight needles

- Toy stuffing

- 2 x 10mm (½in) buttons

- Scrap piece of 4-ply yarn for embroidering nose

Before you start, please read the Essential Notes at the beginning of this book.

SQUIRREL PATTERN

HEAD

Starting at neck:

Using Yarn A and 2.75mm straight needles, cast on 11 sts.

Row 1 (ws): Purl.

Row 2: [K1, M1] to last st, K1. (21 sts)

Row 3: Purl.

Row 4: [K2, M1] to last st, K1. (31 sts)

Row 5: Purl.

Row 6: K1, m1l, knit to last st, m1r, K1. (33 sts)

Row 7: Purl.

Row 8: [K1, m1l, K15, m1r] twice, K1. (37 sts)

Row 9: Purl.

Row 10: [K1, m1l, K17, m1r] twice, K1. (41 sts)

Row 11: P20, m1pl, P1, m1pr, P20. (43 sts)

Row 12: (A) K1, m1l, K20, m1r, (B) K1, (A) m1l, K20, m1r, K1. (47 sts)

Row 13: (A) P23, (B) m1pl, P1, m1pr, (A) P23. (49 sts)

Row 14: (A) K22, (B) K2, m1r, K1, m1l, K2, (A) K22. (51 sts)

Row 15: (A) P21, (B) P9, (A) P21.

Row 16: (A) K1, m1l, K20, (B) K4, m1r, K1, m1l, K4, (A) K20, m1r, K1. (55 sts)

Row 17: (A) P22, (B) P11, (A) P22.

Row 18: (A) K22, (B) K5, sl1, K5, (A) K22.

Row 19: (A) P22, (B) P11, (A) P22.

Row 20: (A) K23, (B) K4, sl1, K4, (A) K23.

Continue in Yarn A only.

Row 21: Purl.

Row 22: K26, CDD, K26. (53 sts)

Row 23: Purl.

Row 24: K25, CDD, K25. (51 sts)

Row 25: Purl.

Row 26: K24, CDD, K24. (49 sts)

Row 27: Purl.

Row 28: K1, K2tog, K20, CDD, K20, SSK, K1. (45 sts)

Row 29: Purl.

Row 30: K21, CDD, K21. (43 sts)

Row 31: Purl.

Row 32: K1, K2tog, K17, CDD, K17, SSK, K1. (39 sts)

Row 33: Purl.

Row 34: K19, sl1, K19.

Row 35: Purl.

Row 36: K1, K2tog, K16, sl1, K16, SSK, K1. (37 sts)

Row 37: Purl.

Row 38: K18, sl1, K18.

Row 39: Purl.

Row 40: K1, K2tog, K3, K2tog 4 times, K3, CDD, K3, SSK 4 times, K3, SSK, K1. (25 sts)

Row 41: Purl.

Row 42: K1, K2tog 5 times, CDD, SSK 5 times, K1. (13 sts)

Row 43: Purl.

Cast off.

EARS (MAKE 2)

Using Yarn A and 2.75mm straight needles, cast on 14 sts.

Row 1 (ws): Purl.

Row 2: K5, [K1, M1] 3 times, knit to end. (17 sts)

Rows 3–7: Stocking stitch 5 rows.

Row 8: [K3, K2tog, SSK] twice, K3. (13 sts)

Row 9: Purl.

Row 10: K1, [K1, K2tog, SSK] twice, K2. (9 sts)

Row 11: Purl.

Row 12: K1, K2tog, sl1 kw, K2tog, PSSO, SSK, K1. (5 sts)

Row 13: Purl.

Row 14: Knit.

Cut yarn leaving a long tail. Using a tapestry needle, thread tail through the stitches left on needle and pull up tight to gather stitches.

TAIL

Using Yarn A and 2.75mm straight needles, cast on 25 sts.

Row 1 (ws): P3, turn.

Row 2: YO, K3.

Row 3: P3, SSP, P1, turn.

Row 4: YO, K5.

Row 5: P5, SSP, P1, turn.

Row 6: YO, K7.

Row 7: P7, SSP, P1, turn.

Row 8: YO, K9.

Row 9: P9, SSP, P1, turn.

Row 10: YO, K11.

Row 11: P11, SSP, purl to end.

Row 12: K3, turn.

Row 13: YO, P3.

Row 14: K3, K2tog, K1, turn.

Row 15: YO, P5.

Row 16: K5, K2tog, K1, turn.

Row 17: YO, P7.

Row 18: K7, K2tog, K1, turn.

Row 19: YO, P9.

Row 20: K9, K2tog, K1, turn.

Row 21: YO, P11.

Row 22: K11, K2tog, knit to end.

Rows 23–66: Rpt Rows 1-22 twice more.

Rows 67–75: Stocking stitch 9 rows.

Row 76: [K1, m1l, K11, m1r] twice, K1. (29 sts)

Rows 77–87: Stocking stitch 11 rows.

Row 88: [K1, m1l, K13, m1r] twice, K1. (33 sts)

Rows 89–99: Stocking stitch 11 rows.

Row 100: [K1, m1l, K15, m1r] twice, K1. (37 sts)

Row 101: Purl.

Row 102: K35, turn.

Row 103: YO, P33, turn.

Row 104: YO, K31, turn.

Row 105: YO, P29, turn.

Row 106: YO, K27, turn.

Row 107: YO, P25, turn.

Row 108: YO, K23, turn.

Row 109: YO, P21, turn.

Row 110: YO, P19, turn.

Row 111: YO, P17, turn.

Row 112: YO, K15, turn.

Row 113: YO, P13, turn.

Row 114: YO, K13, [K2tog, K1] to end.

Row 115: P25, [SSP, P1] to end.

Rows 116–143: Rpt Rows 102-115 twice more.

Rows 144–145: Stocking stitch 2 rows.

Row 146: K1, K2tog, K31, SSK, K1. (35 sts)

Row 147: Purl.

Row 148: K16, CDD, K16. (33 sts)

Row 149: Purl.

Row 150: K1, K2tog, K27, SSK, K1. (31 sts)

Row 151: Purl.

Row 152: K14, CDD, K14. (29 sts)

Row 153: Purl.

Row 154: K1, K2tog, K10, CDD, K10, SSK, K1. (25 sts)

Row 155: Purl.

Row 156: K11, CDD, K11. (23 sts)

Row 157: Purl.

Row 158: K10, CDD, K10. (21 sts)

Row 159: Purl.

Row 160: K9, CDD, K9. (19 sts)

Row 161: P8, PCDD, P8. (17 sts)

Row 162: K7, CDD, K7. (15 sts)

Row 163: P6, PCDD, P6. (13 sts)

Row 164: K5, CDD, K5. (11 sts)

Row 165: P4, PCDD, P4. (9 sts)

Row 166: K3, CDD, K3. (7 sts)

Row 167: P2, PCDD, P2. (5 sts)

Rows 168–169: Stocking stitch 2 rows.

Cut yarn leaving a long tail. Using a tapestry needle, thread tail through the stitches left on needle and pull up tight to gather stitches.

BODY

Work as Standard Body – Contrast Front 1 (see Standard Body Parts).

ARMS (MAKE 2)

Work as Standard Arms (see Standard Body Parts).

LEGS (MAKE 2)

Work as Standard Legs – Plain (see Standard Body Parts).

MAKING UP

Follow the instructions in the techniques section (see Techniques: Making Up Your Animal).

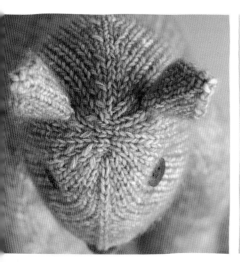

Ella

THE UNICORN

• • • • • • • • • • • • • • • • •

YOU WILL NEED

- Scheepjes Stonewashed (50g/130m; 78% cotton/22% acrylic) yarn in the following shade:

  - **Yarn A** *Cream (Moonstone 801), 2 balls.*

- Scheepjes Twinkle (50g/130m; 75% cotton/25% polyester) yarn in the following shade:

  - **Yarn B** *Pale Gold (938), 1 ball.*

- Scheepjes Catona (25g/62m; 100% cotton) yarn in the following shades:

  - **Yarn C** *Peach (Peach 523), 1 ball.*

  - **Yarn D** *Pink (Soft Rose 409), 1 ball.*

  - **Yarn E** *Yellow (Primrose 522), 1 ball.*

  - **Yarn F** *Light Turquoise (Chrystaline 385), 1 ball.*

  - **Yarn G** *Turquoise (Tropic 253), 1 ball.*

- 2.75mm (US 2) straight needles

- 3mm (US2½) double-pointed needles

- Toy stuffing

- 2 x 10mm (½in) buttons

- Scrap piece of 4-ply yarn for embroidering nostrils

Before you start, please read the Essential Notes at the beginning of this book.

UNICORN PATTERN

HEAD

Cast on 9 sts using 2.75mm needles and Yarn A.

Row 1 (WS): Purl.

Row 2: [K1, M1] 7 times, K2. (16 sts)

Row 3: Purl.

Row 4: K1, M1, [K2, M1] 7 times, K1. (24 sts)

Row 5: Purl.

Row 6: K1, M1, [K3, M1] 7 times, K2. (32 sts)

Row 7: Purl.

Row 8: K1, M1, [K4, M1] 7 times, K3. (40 sts)

Row 9: Purl.

Row 10: K1, M1, [K5, M1] 7 times, K4. (48 sts)

Row 11: Purl.

Row 12: K1, M1, [K6, M1] 7 times, K5. (56 sts)

Row 13: Purl.

Row 14: K1, M1, [K7, M1] 7 times, K6. (64 sts)

Rows 15-24: Stocking stitch 10 rows.

Row 25: P22, P2tog, P16, SSP, P22. (62 sts)

Row 26: K22, SSK, K14, K2tog, K22. (60 sts)

Row 27: P22, P2tog, P12, SSP, P22. (58 sts)

Row 28: K4, K2tog 6 times, K6, SSK, K10, K2tog, K6, SSK 6 times, K4. (44 sts)

Row 29: Purl.

Row 30: K16, SSK, K8, K2tog, K16. (42 sts)

Row 31: Purl.

Row 32: K15, CDD, K6, CDD, K15. (38 sts)

Rows 33-35: Stocking stitch 3 rows.

Row 36: K14, K2tog, K6, SSK, K14. (36 sts)

Row 37: Purl.

Row 38: K1, K2tog 3 times, K22, SSK 3 times, K1. (30 sts)

Row 39: Purl.

Row 40: K10, K2tog, K6, SSK, K10. (28 sts)

Rows 41-43: Stocking stitch 3 rows.

Row 44: [K1, M1] 3 times, K22, [M1, K1] 3 times. (34 sts)

Rows 45-47: Stocking stitch 3 rows.

Row 48: K8, sl1, K16, sl1, K8.

Row 49: Purl.

Row 50: K7, CDD, K14, CDD, K7. (30 sts)

Row 51: Purl.

Row 52: K6, CDD, K12, CDD, K6. (26 sts)

Row 53: Purl.

Row 54: K5, CDD, K10, CDD, K5. (22 sts)

Row 55: Purl.

Row 56: K4, CDD, K8, CDD, K4. (18 sts)

Row 57: Purl.

Row 58: K1, K2tog, CDD, K2tog twice, SSK, CDD, SSK, K1. (9 sts)

Cut yarn leaving a long tail, using a tapestry needle thread tail through the stitches left on needle and draw up.

EARS (MAKE 2)

Cast on 16 sts using 2.75mm needles and Yarn A.

Row 1 (WS): Purl.

Row 2: K6, [K1, M1] 3 times, K6. (19 sts)

Rows 3-9: Stocking stitch 7 rows.

Row 10: K3, K2tog, SSK, K5, K2tog, SSK, K3. (15 sts)

Rows 11-13: Stocking stitch 3 rows.

Row 14: K2, K2tog, SSK, K3, K2tog, SSK, K2. (11 sts)

Row 15: Purl.

Row 16: K1, K2tog, SSK, K1, K2tog, SSK, K1. (7 sts)

Row 17: Purl.

Row 18: K2tog, sl1 kw, K2tog, PSSO, SSK. (3 sts)

Cut yarn leaving a long tail, using a tapestry needle thread tail through the stitches left on needle and draw up.

HORN

Cast on 16 sts using 2.75mm needles and Yarn B.

Row 1 (WS): Purl.

Row 2: Knit.

Rows 3-5: Purl 3 rows.

Row 6: K1, K2tog, knit to last 3 sts, SSK, K1. (14 sts)

Rows 7-22: Rpt rows 3-6, 4 more times. (6 sts)

Row 23: Purl.

Row 24: Knit.

Cut yarn leaving a long tail, using a tapestry needle thread tail through the stitches left on needle and draw up.

MANE

Using 3mm double pointed needles, cast on 4 sts for each i-cord as follows:

Yarn C: make 2 i-cords x 15 rows long, make 1 i-cord x 20 rows long, make 1 i-cord x 26 rows long.

Yarn D: make 2 i-cords x 30 rows long, make 2 i-cords x 32 rows long.

Yarn E: make 4 i-cords x 32 rows long.

Yarn F: make 4 i-cords x 32 rows long.

Yarn G: make 4 i-cords x 32 rows long.

TAIL

Using 3mm double pointed needles, cast on 4 sts for each i-cord as follows:

Yarn C: make 2 i-cords x 30 rows long.

Yarn D: make 2 i-cords x 35 rows long.

Yarn E: make 2 i-cords x 40 rows long.

Yarn F: make 2 i-cords x 45 rows long.

Yarn G: make 2 i-cords x 45 rows long.

BODY

Work as Standard Body – Plain (see Standard Body Parts).

ARMS (MAKE 2)

Work as Standard Arms (see Standard Body Parts).

LEGS (MAKE 2)

Work as Standard Legs – Contrast Foot Pad (see Standard Body Parts).

MAKING UP

Follow the instructions in the techniques section (see Techniques: Making Up Your Animal).

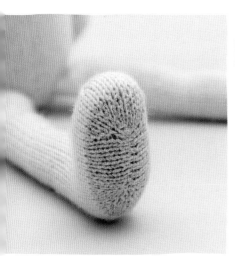

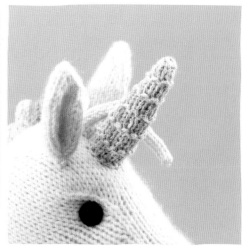

Maisie

THE PIG

YOU WILL NEED

- Scheepjes Stonewashed (50g/130m; 78% cotton/22% acrylic) yarn in the following shades:

  - **Yarn A** *Pale Pink (Pink Quartzite 821), 2 balls*

  - **Yarn B** *Pink (Rose Quartz 820), 1 ball*

- 2.75mm (US 2) straight needles

- Toy stuffing

- 2 x 10mm (½in) buttons

- Scrap piece of 4-ply yarn for embroidering nostrils

Before you start, please read the Essential Notes at the beginning of this book.

PIG PATTERN

HEAD

Starting at neck:

Using Yarn A and 2.75mm straight needles, cast on 11 sts.

Row 1 (ws): Purl.

Row 2: [K1, M1] to last st, K1. (21 sts)

Row 3: Purl.

Row 4: [K2, M1] to last st, K1. (31 sts)

Row 5: Purl.

Row 6: K1, m1l, knit to last st, m1r, K1. (33 sts)

Row 7: P16, P1 and place a removable marker around this stitch on RS, P16.

Row 8: [K1, m1l, K15, m1r] twice, K1. (37 sts)

Row 9: Purl.

Row 10: [K1, m1l, K17, m1r] twice, K1. (41 sts)

Row 11: Purl.

Row 12: [K1, m1l, K19, m1r] twice, K1. (45 sts)

Row 13: Purl.

Row 14: K22, m1r, K1, m1l, K22. (47 sts)

Row 15: Purl.

Row 16: K1, m1l, knit to last st, m1r, K1. (49 sts)

Rows 17–19: Stocking stitch 3 rows.

Row 20: K17, *K1 and place a removable marker around this stitch*, K13, rpt from * to *, K17.

Rows 21–25: Stocking stitch 5 rows.

Row 26: K23, CDD, K23. (47 sts)

Row 27: Purl.

Row 28: K1, K2tog, K19, CDD, K19, SSK, K1. (43 sts)

Row 29: Purl.

Row 30: K20, CDD, K20. (41 sts)

Row 31: P20, P1 and place a removable marker around this stitch on RS, P20.

Row 32: K1, K2tog, K17, sl1, K17, SSK, K1. (39 sts)

Row 33: Purl.

Row 34: K19, sl1, K19.

Row 35: Purl.

Row 36: K1, K2tog, K16, sl1, K16, SSK, K1. (37 sts)

Row 37: Purl.

Row 38: K18, sl1, K18.

Row 39: Purl.

Row 40: K1, K2tog, K3, K2tog 4 times, K3, CDD, K3, SSK 4 times, K3, SSK, K1. (25 sts)

Row 41: Purl.

Row 42: K1, K2tog 5 times, CDD, SSK 5 times, K1. (13 sts)

Row 43: Purl.

Cast off.

SNOUT

Using Yarn A and 2.75mm straight needles, cast on 31 sts.

Row 1 (ws): Purl.

Rows 2-9: Stocking stitch 8 rows.

Row 10: Purl.

Change to Yarn B.

Row 11: Purl.

Row 12: K4, K2tog 4 times, K7, K2tog 4 times, K4. (23 sts)

Row 13: Purl.

Row 14: K4, K2tog twice, K7, K2tog twice, K4. (19 sts)

Row 15: Purl.

Row 16: K2tog 4 times, CDD, K2tog 4 times. (9 sts)

Cut yarn leaving a long tail. Using a tapestry needle, thread tail through the stitches left on needle and pull up tight to gather stitches.

EARS (MAKE 2)

Using Yarn A and 2.75mm straight needles, cast on 33 sts.

Row 1 (ws): (A) P10, (B) P13, (A) P10.

Row 2: (A) K10, (B) K13, (A) K10.

Rows 3–11: Rpt last 2 rows 4 more times, then rpt Row 1 again.

Row 12: (A) K7, K2tog, K1, (B) SSK, K9, K2tog, (A) K1, SSK, K7. (29 sts)

Row 13: (A) P9, (B) P11, (A) P9.

Row 14: (A) K6, K2tog, K1, (B) SSK, K7, K2tog, (A) K1, SSK, K6. (25 sts)

Row 15: (A) P8, (B) P9, (A) P8.

Row 16: (A) K5, K2tog, K1, (B) SSK, K5, K2tog, (A) K1, SSK, K5. (21 sts)

Row 17: (A) P7, (B) P7, (A) P7.

Row 18: (A) K4, K2tog, K1, (B) SSK, K3, K2tog, (A) K1, SSK, K4. (17 sts)

Row 19: (A) P6, (B) P5, (A) P6.

Row 20: (A) K3, K2tog, K1, (B) SSK, K1, K2tog, (A) K1, SSK, K3. (13 sts)

Row 21: (A) P5, (B) P3, (A) P5.

Row 22: (A) K2, K2tog, SSK, (B) K1, (A) K2tog, SSK, K2. (9 sts)

Continue in Yarn A only.

Row 23: Purl.

Row 24: K1, K2tog, K3, SSK, K1. (7 sts)

Cut yarn leaving a long tail. Using a tapestry needle, thread tail through the stitches left on needle and pull up tight to gather stitches.

TAIL

Using Yarn A and 2.75mm straight needles, cast on 16 sts.

Row 1 (ws): Purl.

Rows 2–5: Stocking stitch 4 rows.

Row 6: [K1, K2tog, K2, SSK, K1] twice. (12 sts)

Rows 7–9: Stocking stitch 3 rows.

Row 10: [K1, K2tog, SSK, K1] twice. (8 sts)

Rows 11–13: Stocking stitch 3 rows.

Row 14: K7, turn.

Row 15: YO, P6, turn.

Row 16: YO, K5, turn.

Row 17: YO, P4, turn.

Row 18: YO, K3, turn.

Row 19: YO, P2, turn.

Row 20: YO, K2, K2tog 3 times.

Row 21: P5, SSP 3 times.

Rows 22–69: Rpt Rows 14-21 6 more times.

Rows 70–79: Stocking stitch 10 rows.

Row 80: K1, K2tog 3 times, K1. (5 sts)

Row 81: Purl.

Cut yarn leaving a long tail. Using a tapestry needle, thread tail through the stitches left on needle and pull up tight to gather stitches.

BODY

Work as Standard Body – Plain (see Standard Body Parts).

ARMS (MAKE 2)

Work as Standard Arms (see Standard Body Parts).

LEGS (MAKE 2)

Work as Standard Leg – Plain (see Standard Body Parts).

MAKING UP

Follow the instructions in the techniques section (see Techniques: Making Up Your Animal).

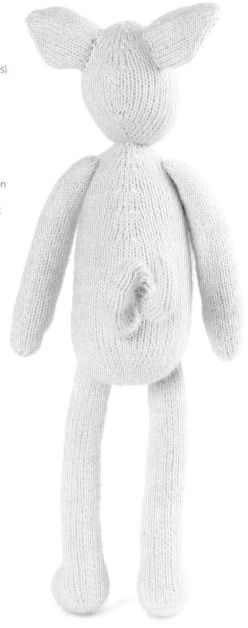

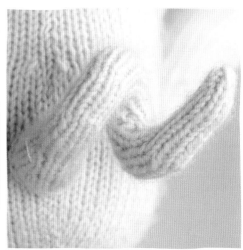

Stanley

THE RACCOON

YOU WILL NEED

- Scheepjes Stonewashed (50g/130m; 78% cotton/22% acrylic) yarn in the following shades:

  - **Yarn A** Grey (Smokey Quartz 802), 2 balls

  - **Yarn B** Cream (Moonstone 801), 1 ball

  - **Yarn C** Black (Black Onyx 803), 1 ball

- 2.75mm (US 2) straight needles

- Toy stuffing

- 2 x 10mm (½in) buttons

- Scrap piece of 4-ply yarn for embroidering nose

Before you start, please read the Essential Notes at the beginning of this book.

RACCOON PATTERN

HEAD

Starting at neck:

Using Yarn A and 2.75mm straight needles, cast on 11 sts.

Row 1 (ws): (A) P4, (B) P3, (A) P4.

Row 2: (A) [K1, M1] 4 times, (B) [K1, M1] 3 times, (A) [K1, M1] 3 times, K1. (21 sts)

Row 3: (A) P7, (B) P6, (A) P8.

Row 4: (A) [K2, M1] 3 times, K2, (B) [M1, K2] 3 times, (A) [M1, K2] 3 times, M1, K1. (31 sts)

Row 5: (A) P11, (B) P9, (A) P11.

Row 6: (A) K1, m1l, K10, (B) K9, (A) K10, m1r, K1. (33 sts)

Row 7: (A) P12, (B) P9, (A) P12.

Row 8: (A) K1, m1l, K10, (B) K5, m1r, K1, m1l, K5, (A) K10, m1r, K1. (37 sts)

Row 9: (A) P12, (B) P13, (A) P12.

Row 10: (A) K1, m1l, K10, (B) K7, m1r, K1, m1l, K7, (A) K10, m1r, K1. (41 sts)

Row 11: (A) P12, (B) P8, m1pl, P1, m1pr, P8, (A) P12. (43 sts)

Row 12: (A) K1, m1l, K10, (B) K10, m1r, K1, m1l, K10, (A) K10, m1r, K1. (47 sts)

Row 13: (A) P12, (B) P11, m1pl, P1, m1pr, P11, (A) P12. (49 sts)

Row 14: (A) K11, (B) K13, m1r, K1, m1l, K13, (A) K11. (51 sts)

Row 15: (A) P11, (B) P14, m1pl, P1, m1pr, P14, (A) P11. (53 sts)

Row 16: (A) K1, m1l, K9, (B) K16, m1r, K1, m1l, K16, (A) K9, m1r, K1. (57 sts)

Row 17: (A) P11, (B) P35, (A) P11.

Row 18: (A) K10, (B) K4, (C) K6, (B) K8, m1r, K1, m1l, K8, (C) K6, (B) K4, (A) K10. (59 sts)

Row 19: (A) P10, (B) P3, (C) P7, (B) P19, (C) P7, (B) P3, (A) P10.

Row 20: (A) K9, (B) K3, (C) K8, (B) K9, sl1, K9, (C) K8, (B) K3, (A) K9.

Row 21: (A) P9, (B) P2, (C) P9, (B) P19, (C) P9, (B) P2, (A) P9.

Row 22: (A) K8, (B) K2, (C) K11, (B) K7, CDD, K7, (C) K11, (B) K2, (A) K8. (57 sts)

Row 23: (A) P8, (B) P2, (C) P11, (B) P15, (C) P11, (B) P2, (A) P8.

Row 24: (A) K9, (B) K2, (C) K10, (B) K6, CDD, K6, (C) K10, (B) K2, (A) K9. (55 sts)

Row 25: (A) P9, (B) P2, (C) P11, (B) P4, PCDD, P4, (C) P11, (B) P2, (A) P9. (53 sts)

Row 26: (A) K10, (B) K2, (C) K10, (B) K3, CDD, K3, (C) K10, (B) K2, (A) K10. (51 sts)

Row 27: (A) P10, (B) P2, (C) P11, (B) P1, PCDD, P1, (C) P11, (B) P2, (A) P10. (49 sts)

Row 28: (A) K1, K2tog, K8, (B) K2, (C) K10, CDD, K10, (B) K2, (A) K8, SSK, K1. (45 sts)

Row 29: (A) P10, (B) P2, (C) P9, PCDD, P9, (B) P2, (A) P10. (43 sts)

Row 30: (A) K11, (B) K2, (C) K7, CDD, K7, (B) K2, (A) K11. (41 sts)

Row 31: (A) P11, (B) P2, (C) P6, (A) P3, (C) P6, (B) P2, (A) P11.

Row 32: (A) K1, K2tog, K9, (B) K2, (C) K5, (A) K1, sl1, K1, (C) K5, (B) K2, (A) K9, SSK, K1. (39 sts)

Row 33: (A) P11, (B) P3, (C) P3, (B) P1, (A) P3, (B) P1, (C) P3, (B) P3, (A) P11.

Row 34: (A) K12, (B) K6, (A) K1, sl1, K1, (B) K6, (A) K12.

Row 35: (A) P12, (B) P6, (A) P3, (B) P6, (A) P12.

Row 36: (A) K1, K2tog, K10, (B) K5, (A) K1, sl1, K1, (B) K5, (A) K10, SSK, K1. (37 sts)

Row 37: (A) P13, (B) P3, (A) P5, (B) P3, (A) P13.

Continue in Yarn A only.

Row 38: K18, sl1, K18.

Row 39: Purl.

Row 40: K1, K2tog, K3, K2tog 4 times, K3, CDD, K3, SSK 4 times, K3, SSK, K1. (25 sts)

Row 41: Purl.

Row 42: K1, K2tog 5 times, CDD, SSK 5 times, K1. (13 sts)

Row 43: Purl.

Cast off.

EARS (MAKE 2)

Using 2.75mm straight needles and Yarn A, cast on 18 sts.

Row 1 (ws): (A) P7, (C) P4, (A) P7.

Row 2: (A) K7, (C) [K1, M1] 3 times, K1, (A) K7. (21 sts)

Row 3: (A) P7, (C) P7, (A) P7.

Row 4: (A) K7, (C) K7, (A) K7.

Row 5: (A) P7, (C) P7, (A) P7.

Row 6: (A) K4, K2tog, K1, (C) SSK, K3, K2tog, (A) K1, SSK, K4. (17 sts)

Row 7: (A) P6, (C) P5, (A) P6.

Row 8: (A) K6, (C) K5, (A) K6.

Row 9: (A) P6, (C) P5, (A) P6.

Row 10: (A) K3, K2tog, K1, (C) SSK, K1, K2tog, (A) K1, SSK, K3. (13 sts)

Row 11: (A) P5, (C) P3, (A) P5.

Continue in Yarn A only.

Row 12: K2, K2tog, SSK, K1, K2tog, SSK, K2. (9 sts)

Row 13: Purl.

Row 14: K1, K2tog, sl1 kw, K2tog, PSSO, SSK, K1. (5 sts)

Cut yarn leaving a long tail. Using a tapestry needle, thread tail through the stitches left on needle and pull up tight to gather stitches.

TAIL

Using 2.75mm straight needles and Yarn A, cast on 19 sts.

Row 1 (ws): Purl.

Rows 2–3: Stocking stitch 2 rows.

Work rows 4–35 in a stripe rpt of 4 rows Yarn C and 4 rows Yarn A, starting with Yarn C.

Rows 4–5: Stocking stitch 2 rows.

Row 6: K4, [M1, K6] twice, M1, K3. (22 sts)

Rows 7–9: Stocking stitch 3 rows.

Row 10: K1, [M1, K7] 3 times. (25 sts)

Rows 11–13: Stocking stitch 3 rows.

Row 14: K3, [M1, K4] 5 times, M1, K2. (31 sts)

Rows 15–33: Stocking stitch 19 rows.

Row 34: K6, SSK, K1, K2tog, K20. (29 sts)

Row 35: Purl.

Continue in Yarn C only.

Row 36: K19, SSK, K1, K2tog, K5. (27 sts)

Row 37: Purl.

Row 38: K5, SSK, K1, K2tog, K17. (25 sts)

Row 39: Purl.

Row 40: [K4, SSK, K1, K2tog, K3] twice, K1. (21 sts)

Row 41: Purl.

Row 42: [K3, SSK, K1, K2tog, K2] twice, K1. (17 sts)

Row 43: Purl.

Row 44: [K2, SSK, K1, K2tog, K1] twice, K1. (13 sts)

Row 45: Purl.

Row 46: [K1, SSK, K1, K2tog] twice, K1. (9 sts)

Row 47: Purl.

Row 48: SSK, K1, K2tog, CDD, K1. (5 sts)

Row 49: Purl.

Cut yarn leaving a long tail. Using a tapestry needle, thread tail through the stitches left on needle and pull up tight to gather stitches.

BODY

Work as Standard Body – Chest Blaze (see Standard Body Parts).

ARMS (MAKE 2)

Work as Standard Arms (see Standard Body Parts).

LEGS (MAKE 2)

Work as Standard Leg – Contrast Foot Pad, but using Yarn C instead of Yarn B for Rows 1–8 (see Standard Body Parts).

MAKING UP

Follow the instructions in the techniques section (see Techniques: Making Up Your Animal).

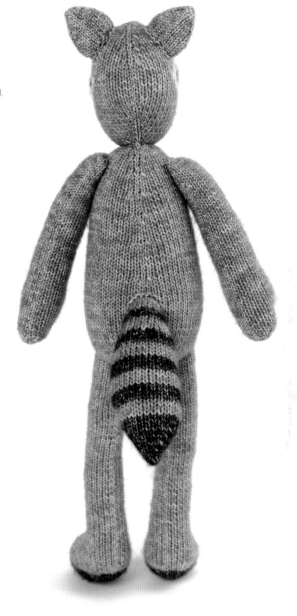

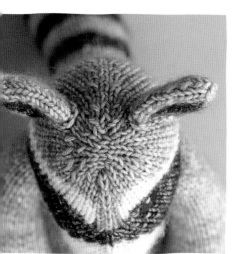

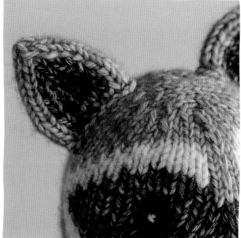

Tilly
THE HARE

• • • • • • • • • • • • • • • • • • •

YOU WILL NEED

- Scheepjes Stonewashed (50g/130m;
78% cotton/22% acrylic) yarn
in the following shades:

  - **Yarn A** *Ecru (Axinite 831), 2 balls*

  - **Yarn B** *Cream (Moonstone 801), 1 ball*

- 2.75mm (US 2) straight needles

- Toy stuffing

- 2 x 10mm (½in) buttons

- Scrap piece of 4-ply yarn for
embroidering nose

- 35mm (1⅜in) pompom maker

*Before you start, please read the Essential Notes at the
beginning of this book.*

HARE PATTERN

HEAD

Starting at neck:

Using 2.75mm straight needles and Yarn A, cast on 11 sts.

Row 1 (ws): Purl.

Row 2: [K1, M1] to last st, K1. (21 sts)

Row 3: Purl.

Row 4: [K2, M1] to last st, K1. (31 sts)

Row 5: Purl.

Row 6: K1, m1l, knit to last st, m1r, K1. (33 sts)

Row 7: Purl.

Row 8: [K1, m1l, K15, m1r] twice, K1. (37 sts)

Row 9: Purl.

Row 10: [K1, m1l, K17, m1r] twice, K1. (41 sts)

Row 11: P20, m1pl, P1, m1pr, P20. (43 sts)

Row 12: [K1, m1l, K20, m1r] twice, K1. (47 sts)

Row 13: P23, m1pl, P1, m1pr, P23. (49 sts)

Row 14: K24, m1r, K1, m1l, K24. (51 sts)

Row 15: Purl.

Row 16: [K1, m1l, K24, m1r] twice, K1. (55 sts)

Row 17: Purl.

Row 18: K27, sl1, K27.

Rows 19–21: Rpt last 2 rows once more, then rpt Row 17 again.

Row 22: K26, CDD, K26. (53 sts)

Row 23: Purl.

Row 24: K25, CDD, K25. (51 sts)

Row 25: P24, PCDD, P24. (49 sts)

Row 26: K23, CDD, K23. (47 sts)

Row 27: Purl.

Row 28: K1, K2tog, K19, CDD, K19, SSK, K1. (43 sts)

Row 29: Purl.

Row 30: K20, CDD, K20. (41 sts)

Row 31: Purl.

Row 32: K1, K2tog, K17, sl1, K17, SSK, K1. (39 sts)

Row 33: Purl.

Row 34: K19, sl1, K19.

Row 35: Purl.

Row 36: K1, K2tog, K16, sl1, K16, SSK, K1. (37 sts)

Row 37: Purl.

Row 38: K18, sl1, K18.

Row 39: Purl.

Row 40: K1, K2tog, K3, K2tog 4 times, K3, CDD, K3, SSK 4 times, K3, SSK, K1. (25 sts)

Row 41: Purl.

Row 42: K1, K2tog 5 times, CDD, SSK 5 times, K1. (13 sts)

Row 43: Purl.

Cast off.

EARS (MAKE 2)

Using 2.75mm straight needles and Yarn A, cast on 15 sts.

Row 1 (ws): (A) P6, (B) P3, (A) P6.

Row 2: (A) K6, (B) [K1, M1] 3 times, (A) K6. (18 sts)

Row 3: (A) P6, (B) P6, (A) P6.

Row 4: (A) K6, (B) K6, (A) K6.

Row 5: (A) P6, (B) P6, (A) P6.

Row 6: (A) K4, m1r, K2, (B) K1, m1l, K4, m1r, K1, (A) K2, m1l, K4. (22 sts)

Row 7: (A) P7, (B) P8, (A) P7.

Row 8: (A) K7, (B) K8, (A) K7.

Row 9: (A) P7, (B) P8, (A) P7.

Row 10: (A) K5, m1r, K2, (B) K1, m1l, K6, m1r, K1, (A) K2, m1l, K5. (26 sts)

Row 11: (A) P8, (B) P10, (A) P8.

Row 12: (A) K8, (B) K10, (A) K8.

Rows 13–15: Rpt last 2 rows once more, then rpt Row 11 again.

Row 16: (A) K6, m1r, K2, (B) K1, m1l, K8, m1r, K1, (A) K2, m1l, K6. (30 sts)

Row 17: (A) P9, (B) P12, (A) P9.

Row 18: (A) K9, (B) K12, (A) K9.

Rows 19–27: Rpt last 2 rows 4 more times, then rpt Row 17 again.

Row 28: (A) K6, K2tog, K1, (B) SSK, K8, K2tog, (A) K1, SSK, K6. (26 sts)

Row 29: (A) P8, (B) P10, (A) P8.

Row 30: (A) K8, (B) K10, (A) K8.

Row 31: (A) P8, (B) P10, (A) P8.

Row 32: (A) K5, K2tog, K1, (B) SSK, K6, K2tog, (A) K1, SSK, K5. (22 sts)

Rows 33–35: Rpt Rows 7–9.

Row 36: (A) K4, K2tog, K1, (B) SSK, K4, K2tog, (A) K1, SSK, K4. (18 sts)

Rows 37–39: Rpt Rows 3–5.

Row 40: (A) K3, K2tog, K1, (B) SSK, K2, K2tog, (A) K1, SSK, K3. (14 sts)

Row 41: (A) P5, (B) P4, (A) P5.

Row 42: (A) K2, K2tog, K1, (B) SSK, K2tog, (A) K1, SSK, K2. (10 sts)

Row 43: (A) P4, (B) P2, (A) P4.

Cut Yarn B leaving a long tail and continue in Yarn A.

Row 44: K1, [K2tog, SSK] twice, K1. (6 sts)

Row 45: Purl.

Cut yarn leaving a long tail. Using a tapestry needle, thread tail through the stitches left on needle and pull up tight to gather stitches.

TAIL

Using Yarn B make a pompom approximately 35mm (1⅜in) diameter.

BODY

Work as Standard Body – Plain (see Standard Body Parts).

ARMS (MAKE 2)

Work as Standard Arms (see Standard Body Parts).

LEGS (MAKE 2)

Work as Standard Legs – Contrast Foot Pad (see Standard Body Parts).

MAKING UP

Follow the instructions in the techniques section (see Techniques: Making Up Your Animal).

Amelia

THE DUCK

YOU WILL NEED

- Scheepjes Stonewashed (50g/130m; 78% cotton/22% acrylic) yarn in the following shades:

  - **Yarn A** *Cream (Moonstone 801), 2 balls*

  - **Yarn B** *Orange (Coral 816), 1 ball*

- 2.75mm (US 2) straight needles

- Toy stuffing

- 2 x 10mm (½in) buttons

Before you start, please read the Essential Notes at the beginning of this book.

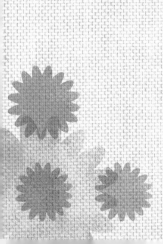

DUCK PATTERN

HEAD

Starting at neck:

Using 2.75mm straight needles and Yarn A, cast on 11 sts.

Row 1 (ws): Purl.

Row 2: [K1, M1] to last st, K1. (21 sts)

Row 3: Purl.

Row 4: [K2, M1] to last st, K1. (31 sts)

Row 5: Purl.

Row 6: K1, m1l, knit to last st, m1r, K1. (33 sts)

Row 7: Purl.

Row 8: [K1, m1l, K15, m1r] twice, K1. (37 sts)

Row 9: Purl.

Row 10: [K1, m1l, K17, m1r] twice, K1. (41 sts)

Row 11: P20, P1 and place a removable marker around this stitch on RS, P20.

Row 12: [K1, m1l, K19, m1r] twice, K1. (45 sts)

Row 13: Purl.

Row 14: K22, m1r, K1, m1l, K22. (47 sts)

Row 15: Purl.

Row 16: K1, m1l, knit to last st, m1r, K1. (49 sts)

Row 17: Purl.

Row 18: K18, *K1 and place a removable marker around this stitch*, K11; rpt from * to *, K18.

Rows 19–25: Stocking stitch 7 rows.

Row 26: K23, CDD, K23. (47 sts)

Row 27: Purl.

Row 28: K1, K2tog, K19, CDD, K19, SSK, K1. (43 sts)

Row 29: Purl.

Row 30: K20, CDD, K20. (41 sts)

Row 31: P20, P1 and place a removable marker around this stitch on RS, P20.

Row 32: K1, K2tog, K17, sl1, K17, SSK, K1. (39 sts)

Row 33: Purl.

Row 34: K19, sl1, K19.

Row 35: Purl.

Row 36: K1, K2tog, K16, sl1, K16, SSK, K1. (37 sts)

Row 37: Purl.

Row 38: K18, sl1, K18.

Row 39: Purl.

Row 40: K1, K2tog, K3, K2tog 4 times, K3, CDD, K3, SSK 4 times, K3, SSK, K1. (25 sts)

Row 41: Purl.

Row 42: K1, K2tog 5 times, CDD, SSK 5 times, K1. (13 sts)

Row 43: Purl.

Cast off.

BEAK

Using 2.75mm straight needles and Yarn B, cast on 33 sts.

Row 1 (ws): Purl.

Row 2: K6, sl1, K8, CDD, K8, sl1, K6. (31 sts)

Row 3: Purl.

Row 4: K6, sl1, K7, CDD, K7, sl1, K6. (29 sts)

Row 5: Purl.

Row 6: K6, sl1, K15, sl1, K6.

Rows 7–19: Rpt last 2 rows 6 more times, then rpt Row 5 again.

Row 20: K5, CDD, K13, CDD, K5. (25 sts)

Row 21: Purl.

Row 22: K4, CDD, K11, CDD, K4. (21 sts)

Row 23: P3, PCDD, P9, PCDD, P3. (17 sts)

Row 24: K2, CDD, K7, CDD, K2. (13 sts)

Cut yarn leaving a long tail. Using a tapestry needle, thread tail through the stitches left on needle and pull up tight to gather stitches.

TAIL

Using 2.75mm straight needles and Yarn A, cast on 27 sts.

Row 1 (ws): P18, turn.

Row 2: YO, K9, turn.

Row 3: YO, P9, SSP, P1, turn.

Row 4: YO, K11, K2tog, K1, turn.

Row 5: YO, P13, SSP, P1, turn.

Row 6: YO, K15, K2tog, K1, turn.

Row 7: YO, P17, SSP, P1, turn.

Row 8: YO, K19, K2tog, K1, turn.

Row 9: YO, P21, SSP, purl to end.

Row 10: K24, K2tog, knit to end.

Rows 11–13: Stocking stitch 3 rows.

Row 14: K1, K2tog, K21, SSK, K1. (25 sts)

Row 15: Purl.

Row 16: [K1, K2tog, K7, SSK] twice, K1. (21 sts)

Row 17: Purl.

Row 18: K1, K2tog, K15, SSK, K1. (19 sts)

Row 19: Purl.

Row 20: [K1, K2tog, K4, SSK] twice, K1. (15 sts)

Row 21: Purl.

Row 22: [K1, K2tog, K2, SSK] twice, K1. (11 sts)

Row 23: Purl.

Row 24: K1, K2tog, K1, CDD, K1, SSK, K1. (7 sts)

Rows 25–28: Stocking stitch 4 rows.

Cut yarn leaving a long tail. Using a tapestry needle, thread tail through the stitches left on needle and pull up tight to gather stitches.

BODY

Work as Standard Body – Plain (see Standard Body Parts).

ARMS (MAKE 2)

Work as Standard Arms (see Standard Body Parts).

LEGS (MAKE 2)

Work as Standard Leg – Contrast Foot Pad (see Standard Body Parts).

MAKING UP

Follow the instructions in the techniques section (see Techniques: Making Up Your Animal).

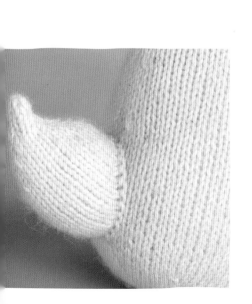

Harry

THE RAM

• • • • • • • • • • • • • • •

YOU WILL NEED

- Scheepjes Stonewashed (50g/130m;
  78% cotton/22% acrylic) yarn
  in the following shades:

  - *Yarn A* Cream (Moonstone 801), 1 ball

  - *Yarn B* Ecru (Axinite 831), 2 balls

  - *Yarn C* Brown (Boulder Opal 804), 1 ball

- 2.75mm (US 2) straight needles

- Toy stuffing

- 2 x 10mm (½in) buttons

- Scrap piece of 4-ply yarn for
  embroidering nose

*Before you start, please read the Essential Notes
at the beginning of this book.*

RAM PATTERN

For 'MB' (make bobble), cast on 2 sts using the Knit cast-on method (see Techniques: Casting On and Stitches), then knit 3 sts casting off the first 2 sts as you work them.

HEAD

Starting at neck:

Using 2.75mm straight needles and Yarn B, cast on 11 sts.

Row 1 (ws): Purl.

Row 2: [K1, M1] to last st, K1. (21 sts)

Row 3: Purl.

Row 4: [K2, M1] to last st, K1. (31 sts)

Row 5: (B) P14, (A) P3, (B) P14.

Row 6: (B) [MB, K1] 7 times, (A) K1, m1r, K1, m1l, K1, (B) [K1, MB] 6 times, K2. (33 sts)

Row 7: (B) P1, m1pr, P13, (A) P5, (B) P13, m1pl, P1. (35 sts)

Row 8: (B) [MB, K1] 7 times, (A) K3, m1r, K1, m1l, K3, (B) [K1, MB] 6 times, K2. (37 sts)

Row 9: (B) P1, m1pr, P13, (A) P4, m1pl, P1, m1pr, P4, (B) P13, m1pl, P1. (41 sts)

Row 10: (B) [MB, K1] 7 times, MB, (A) K5, m1r, K1, m1l, K5, (B) [MB, K1] 7 times, K1. (43 sts)

Row 11: (B) P1, m1pr, P13, (A) P7, m1pl, P1, m1pr, P7, (B) P13, m1pl, P1. (47 sts)

Row 12: (B) [MB, K1] 7 times, MB, (A) K8, m1r, K1, m1l, K8, (B) [MB, K1] 7 times, K1. (49 sts)

Row 13: (B) P1, m1pr, P14, (A) P9, m1pl, P1, m1pr, P9, (B) P14, m1pl, P1. (53 sts)

Row 14: (B) [MB, K1] 8 times, (A) K10, m1r, K1, m1l, K10, (B) [K1, MB] 7 times, K2. (55 sts)

Row 15: (B) P16, (A) P23, (B) P16.

Row 16: (B) [K1, MB] 8 times, (A) K11, m1r, K1, m1l, K11, (B) [MB, K1] 8 times. (57 sts)

Row 17: (B) P1, m1pr, P15, (A) P25, (B) P15, m1pl, P1. (59 sts)

Row 18: (B) [K1, MB] 8 times, (A) K13, sl1, K13, (B) [MB, K1] 8 times.

Row 19: (B) P16, (A) P27, (B) P16.

Row 20: (B) [MB, K1] 7 times, (A) K15, sl1, K15, (B) [K1, MB] 6 times, K2.

Row 21: (B) P14, (A) P31, (B) P14.

Row 22: (B) [K1, MB] 6 times, K1, (A) K16, sl1, K16, (B) [K1, MB] 6 times, K1.

Row 23: (B) P13, (A) P15, PCDD, P15, (B) P13. (57 sts)

Row 24: (B) [MB, K1] 6 times, MB, (A) K15, sl1, K15, (B) [MB, K1] 6 times, K1.

Row 25: (B) P13, (A) P14, PCDD, P14, (B) P13. (55 sts)

Row 26: (B) [K1, MB] 6 times, K1, (A) K13, CDD, K13, (B) [K1, MB] 6 times, K1. (53 sts)

Row 27: (B) P13, (A) P12, PCDD, P12, (B) P13. (51 sts)

Row 28: (B) [MB, K1] 6 times, MB, (A) K11, CDD, K11, (B) [MB, K1] 6 times, K1. (49 sts)

Row 29: (B) P1, SSP, P10, (A) P10, PCDD, P10, (B) P10, P2tog, P1. (45 sts)

Row 30: (B) [MB, K1] 6 times, (A) K9, CDD, K9, (B) [K1, MB] 5 times, K2. (43 sts)

Row 31: (B) P12, (A) P8, PCDD, P8, (B) P12. (41 sts)

Row 32: (B) [K1, MB] 6 times, K1, (A) K5, (B) [K1, MB] twice, K1, (A) K5, (B) [K1, MB] 6 times, K1.

Row 33: (B) P1, SSP, P10, (A) P4, (B) P7, (A) P4, (B) P10, P2tog, P1. (39 sts)

Continue in Yarn B only.

Row 34: [K1, MB] to last st, K1.

Row 35: Purl.

Row 36: [MB, K1] to last st, K1.

Row 37: P1, SSP, P33, P2tog, P1. (37 sts)

Row 38: [MB, K1] to last st, K1.

Row 39: Purl.

Row 40: [K1, MB] to last st, K1.

Row 41: P1, SSP, P3, SSP 4 times, P3, PCDD, P3, P2tog 4 times, P3, P2tog, P1. (25 sts)

Row 42: [K1, MB] to last st, K1.

Row 43: P1, SSP 5 times, PCDD, P2tog 5 times, P1. (13 sts)

Cast off.

EARS (MAKE 2)

Using 2.75mm straight needles and Yarn A, cast on 14 sts.

Row 1 (ws): Purl.

Row 2: K5, [K1, M1] 3 times, knit to end. (17 sts)

Rows 3–7: Stocking stitch 5 rows.

Row 8: [K3, K2tog, SSK] twice, K3. (13 sts)

Row 9: Purl.

Row 10: K1, [K1, K2tog, SSK] twice, K2. (9 sts)

Row 11: Purl.

Row 12: K1, K2tog, sl1 kw, K2tog, PSSO, SSK, K1. (5 sts)

Row 13: Purl.

Cut yarn leaving a long tail. Using a tapestry needle, thread tail through the stitches left on needle and pull up tight to gather stitches.

HORNS (MAKE 2)

Using 2.75mm straight needles and Yarn C, cast on 18 sts.

Row 1 (ws): P12, turn.

Row 2: YO, K6, turn.

Row 3: YO, P6, SSP, P1, turn.

Row 4: YO, K8, K2tog, K1, turn.

Row 5: YO, P10, SSP, P1, turn.

Row 6: YO, K12, K2tog, K1, turn.

Row 7: YO, P14, SSP, P to end.

Row 8: K16, K2tog, K1. (18 sts)

Row 9: Knit.

Row 10: K16, turn.

Row 11: YO, P14, turn.

Row 12: YO, P12, turn.

Row 13: YO, P10, turn.

Row 14: YO, K8, turn.

Row 15: YO, P6, turn.

Row 16: YO, K6, [K2tog, K1] 3 times.

Row 17: P12, (SSP, P1) 3 times. (18 sts)

Row 18: Purl.

Row 19: P16, turn.

Row 20: K14, turn.

Row 21: P12, turn.

Row 22: YO, K10, turn.

Row 23: YO, P8, turn.

Row 24: YO, K6, turn.

Row 25: YO, P6, SSP, P1, SSP twice, P1.

Row 26: K11, K2tog, K1, K2tog twice, K1. (16 sts)

Row 27: Knit.

Row 28: K14, turn.

Row 29: P12, turn.

Row 30: K10, turn.

Row 31: YO, P8, turn.

Row 32: YO, K6, turn.

Row 33: YO, P4, turn.

Row 34: YO, K4, K2tog, K1, K2tog twice, K1.

Row 35: P9, SSP, P1, SSP twice, P1. (14 sts)

Row 36: Purl.

Row 37: P12, turn.

Row 38: K10, turn.

Row 39: P8, turn.

Row 40: YO, K6, turn.

Row 41: YO, P6, SSP twice, P1.

Row 42: K9, K2tog twice, K1. (12 sts)

Row 43: Knit.

Row 44: K10, turn.

Row 45: P8, turn.

Row 46: K6, turn.

Row 47: YO, P4, turn.

Row 48: YO, K4, K2tog twice, K1.

Row 49: P7, SSP twice, P1. (10 sts)

Row 50: Purl.

Row 51: P8, turn.

Row 52: K6, turn.

Row 53: P4, turn.

Row 54: YO, K2, turn.

Row 55: YO, P2, SSP twice, P1.

Row 56: K5, K2tog twice, K1. (8 sts)

Row 57–58: Knit 2 rows.

Row 59: Purl.

Row 60: K2, K2tog, SSK, K2. (6 sts)

Row 61: Purl.

Row 62: K1, K2tog, SSK, K1. (4 sts)

Row 63: Purl.

Cut yarn leaving a long tail. Using a tapestry needle, thread tail through the stitches left on needle and pull up tight to gather stitches.

BODY

Using 2.75mm straight needles and Yarn B, cast on 8 sts.

Rows 1–15: As Rows 1–15 of Standard Body – Plain.

Row 16: [K16, M1] 3 times, K to end. (60 sts)

Row 17: P18, K10, P4, K10, P to end. (The knit stitches on this row mark the leg positions.)

Row 18: [K1, MB] 9 times, K10, [K1, MB] twice, K10, [K1, MB] 8 times, K2.

Row 19: Purl.

Row 20: K2, [MB, K1] to end.

Row 21: Purl.

Row 22: [K1, MB] to last 2 sts, K2.

Rows 23–34: Rpt last 4 rows 3 more times.

Row 35: P1, SSP, P14, SSP twice, P18, SSP twice, P14, SSP, P1. (54 sts)

Row 36: [K1, MB] to last 2 sts, K2.

Rows 37–40: Rpt Rows 19–22.

Rows 41–42: Rpt Rows 19–20.

Row 43: P1, P2tog, P12, P2tog twice, P16, P2tog twice, P12, P2tog, P1. (48 sts)

Rows 44–46: Rpt Rows 20–22.

Rows 47–48: Rpt Rows 19–20.

Row 49: P1, P2tog, P10, P2tog twice, P14, P2tog twice, P10, P2tog, P1. (42 sts)

Rows 50–52: Rpt Rows 20–22.

Rows 53–54: Rpt Rows 19–20.

Row 55: P1, P2tog, P8, P2tog twice, P12, P2tog twice, P8, P2tog, P1. (36 sts)

Rows 56–58: Rpt Rows 20–22.

Row 59: P1, SSP, P6, SSP twice, P10, SSP twice, P6, SSP, P1. (30 sts)

Row 60: As Row 22.

Rows 61–62: Rpt Rows 19–20.

Row 63: P1, P2tog, P4, P2tog twice, P8, P2tog twice, P4, P2tog, P1. (24 sts)

Rows 64–65: Rpt Rows 20–21.

Row 66: K1, [K1, K2tog] to last 2 sts, K2. (17 sts)

Row 67: Purl.

Row 68: K2tog to last st, K1. (9 sts)

Row 69: Purl.

Cut yarn leaving a long tail. Using a tapestry needle, thread tail through the stitches left on needle and pull up tight to gather stitches.

ARMS (MAKE 2)

Work as Standard Arms (see Standard Body Parts).

LEGS (MAKE 2)

Work as Standard Legs – Plain (see Standard Body Parts).

MAKING UP

Follow the instructions in the techniques section (see Techniques: Making Up Your Animal).

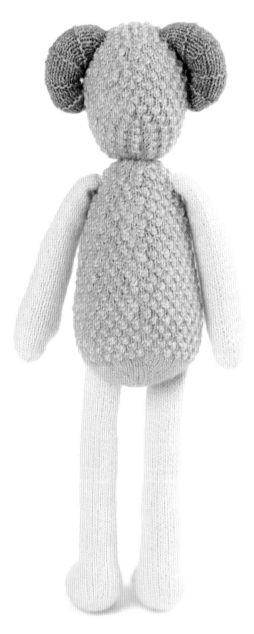

Louis

THE OWL

• • • • • • • • • • • • • • •

YOU WILL NEED

• Scheepjes Stonewashed (50g/130m;
  78% cotton/22% acrylic) yarn
  in the following shades:

  - *Yarn A* Grey (Smokey Quartz 802), 2 balls

  - *Yarn B* Cream (Moonstone 801), 1 ball

  - *Yarn C* Mustard (Yellow Jasper 809), 1 ball

• 2.75mm (US 2) straight needles

• Toy stuffing

• 2 x 10mm (½in) buttons

*Before you start, please read the Essential Notes at the
beginning of this book.*

OWL PATTERN

HEAD

Starting at neck:

Using 2.75mm straight needles and Yarn A, cast on 11 sts.

Row 1 (ws): Purl.

Row 2: [K1, M1] to last st, K1. (21 sts)

Row 3: Purl.

Row 4: [K2, M1] to last st, K1. (31 sts)

Row 5: Purl.

Row 6: K1, m1l, K6, m1r, K1, m1l, K7, sl1, K7, m1r, K1, m1l, K6, m1r, K1. (37 sts)

Row 7: Purl.

Row 8: K1, m1l, K8, m1r, K1, m1l, K8, sl1, K8, m1r, K1, m1l, K8, m1r, K1. (43 sts)

Row 9: Purl.

Row 10: K1, m1l, K10, m1r, K1, m1l, K9, sl1, K9, m1r, K1, m1l, K10, m1r, K1. (49 sts)

Row 11: Purl.

Row 12: K1, m1l, K12, m1r, K1, m1l, K10, sl1, K10, m1r, K1, m1l, K12, m1r, K1. (55 sts)

Row 13: Purl.

Row 14: (A) K21, (B) K6, sl1, K6, (A) K21.

Row 15: (A) P19, (B) P17, (A) P19.

Row 16: (A) K1, m1l, K14, m1r, K1, m1l, K2, (B) K19, (A) K2, m1r, K1, m1l, K14, m1r, K1. (61 sts)

Row 17: (A) P21, (B) P19, (A) P21.

Row 18: (A) K20, (B) K21, (A) K20.

Row 19: (A) P20, (B) P21, (A) P20.

Row 20: (A) K19, (B) K23, (A) K19.

Row 21: (A) P19, (B) P23, (A) P19.

Rows 22–26: Rpt last 2 rows twice more, then rpt Row 20 again.

Row 27: (A) P20, (B) P10, (A) P1, (B) P10, (A) P20.

Row 28: (A) K1, K2tog, K13, CDD, K1, (B) K10, sl1, K10, (A) K1, CDD, K13, SSK, K1. (55 sts)

Row 29: (A) P18, (B) P8, (A) P3, (B) P8, (A) P18.

Row 30: (A) K18, (B) K8, (A) K1, sl1, K1, (B) K8, (A) K18.

Row 31: (A) P19, (B) P6, (A) P5, (B) P6, (A) P19.

Row 32: (A) K1, K2tog, K11, CDD, K3, (B) K4, (A) K3, sl1, K3, (B) K4, (A) K3, CDD, K11, SSK, K1. (49 sts)

Continue in Yarn A only.

Row 33: Purl.

Row 34: K24, sl1, K24.

Row 35: Purl.

Row 36: K1, K2tog, K9, CDD, K9, sl1, K9, CDD, K9, SSK, K1. (43 sts)

Row 37: Purl.

Row 38: K1, K2tog, K7, CDD, K8, sl1, K8, CDD, K7, SSK, K1. (37 sts)

Row 39: Purl.

Row 40: K1, K2tog, K3, K2tog 4 times, K3, CDD, K3, SSK 4 times, K3, SSK, K1. (25 sts)

Row 41: Purl.

Row 42: K1, K2tog 5 times, CDD, SSK 5 times, K1. (13 sts)

Row 43: Purl.

Cast off.

BEAK

Using 2.75mm straight needles and Yarn C, cast on 11 sts.

Row 1 (ws): P7, turn.

Row 2: YO, K3, turn.

Row 3: YO, P3, SSP, P1, turn.

Row 4: YO, K5, K2tog, K1, turn.

Row 5: YO, P7, SSP, P1.

Row 6: K4, CDD, K2, K2tog, K1. (9 sts)

Row 7: Purl.

Row 8: K3, CDD, K3. (7 sts)

Row 9: P2, PCDD, P2. (5 sts)

Cut yarn leaving a long tail. Using a tapestry needle, thread tail through the stitches left on needle and pull up tight to gather stitches.

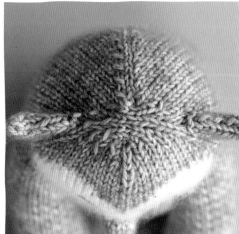

EARS (MAKE 2)

Using 2.75mm straight needles and Yarn A, cast on 17 sts.

Row 1 (ws): Purl.

Row 2: [K3, K2tog, SSK] twice, K3. (13 sts)

Row 3: Purl.

Row 4: K1, [K1, K2tog, SSK] twice, K2. (9 sts)

Row 5: Purl.

Row 6: K1, K2tog, sl1 kw, K2tog, PSSO, SSK, K1. (5 sts)

Row 7: Purl.

Row 8: Knit.

Cut yarn leaving a long tail. Using a tapestry needle, thread tail through the stitches left on needle and pull up tight to gather stitches.

BODY

Work as Standard Body – Contrast Front 1 (see Standard Body Parts).

ARMS (MAKE 2)

Work as Standard Arms (see Standard Body Parts).

LEGS (MAKE 2)

Work as Standard Leg – Plain (see Standard Body Parts).

MAKING UP

Follow the instructions in the techniques section (see Techniques: Making Up Your Animal).

Olivia

THE ELEPHANT

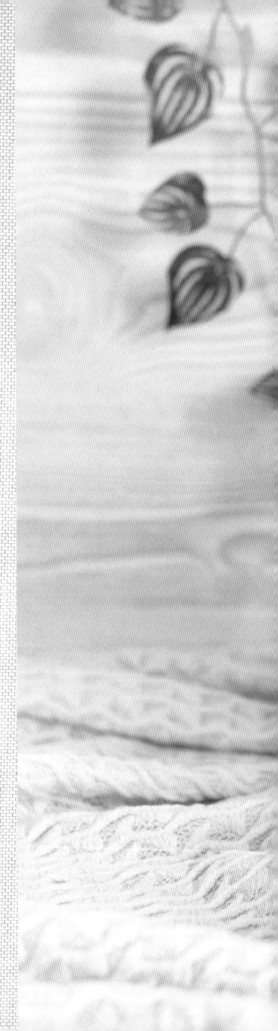

YOU WILL NEED

Please read Tools and Materials at the beginning of the book.

- Scheepjes Stonewashed (50g/130m; 78% cotton/22% acrylic) yarn in the following shade:

  - **Yarn A** *Grey (Smokey Quartz 802); 2 balls.*

- 2.75mm (US 2) straight needles

- Toy stuffing

- 2 x 10mm (½in) buttons

- Extra strong sewing thread

Before you start, please read the Essential Notes at the beginning of this book.

ELEPHANT PATTERN

HEAD

Using 2.75mm straight needles and Yarn A, cast on 9 sts.

Row 1 (WS): Purl.

Row 2: [K1, M1] 7 times, K2. (16 sts)

Row 3: Purl.

Row 4: K1, M1, [K2, M1] 7 times, K1. (24 sts)

Row 5: Purl.

Row 6: K1, M1, [K3, M1] 7 times, K2. (32 sts)

Row 7: Purl.

Row 8: K1, M1, [K4, M1] 7 times, K3. (40 sts)

Row 9: Purl.

Row 10: K1, M1, [K5, M1] 7 times, K4. (48 sts)

Row 11: Purl.

Row 12: K1, M1, [K6, M1] 7 times, K5. (56 sts)

Row 13: Purl.

Row 14: K1, M1, [K7, M1] 7 times, K6. (64 sts)

Rows 15-25: Stocking stitch 11 rows.

Row 26: K4, [SSK, K1] 6 times, CDD, K14, CDD, [K1, K2tog] 6 times, K4. (48 sts)

Row 27: Purl.

Row 28: K15, CDD, K12, CDD, K15. (44 sts)

Row 29: Purl.

Row 30: K14, CDD, K10, CDD, K14. (40 sts)

Row 31: Purl.

Row 32: K13, CDD, K8, CDD, K13. (36 sts)

Row 33: Purl.

Row 34: K12, CDD, K6, CDD, K12. (32 sts)

Row 35: Purl.

Row 36: K11, K2tog, K6, SSK, K11. (30 sts)

Row 37: Purl.

Row 38: K1, K2tog, K7, K2tog, K6, SSK, K7, SSK, K1. (26 sts)

Row 39: Purl.

Row 40: [K1, K2tog] twice, K2tog twice, K6, SSK twice, [SSK, K1] twice. (18 sts)

Row 41: Purl.

Row 42 (short row): K16, turn.

Row 43 (short row): YO, P14, turn. (19 sts)

Row 44 (short row): YO, K14, K2tog, K1, turn. (19 sts)

Row 45: P16, SSP, P1. (18 sts)

Row 46: Knit.

Row 47: Purl.

Rows 48-59: Rpt rows 42-47 twice more.

Rows 60-63: Rpt rows 42-45 once more.

Row 64: K1, K2tog, K12, SSK, K1. (16 sts)

Row 65: Purl.

Row 66 (short row): K14, turn.

Row 67 (short row): YO, P12, turn. (17 sts)

Row 68 (short row): YO, K12, K2tog, K1, turn. (17 sts)

Row 69: P14, SSP, P1. (16 sts)

Row 70: Knit.

Row 71: Purl.

Rows 72-77: Rpt rows 66-71 once more.

Rows 78-81: Rpt rows 66-69 once more.

Row 82: K1, K2tog, K10, SSK, K1. (14 sts)

Row 83: Purl.

Row84 (short row): K12, turn.

Row 85 (short row): YO, P10, turn. (15 sts)

Row 86 (short row): YO, K10, K2tog, K1, turn. (15 sts)

Row 87: P12, SSP, P1. (14 sts)

Rows 88-93: Stocking stitch 6 rows.

Row 94: K2tog to end. (7 sts)

Cut yarn leaving a long tail, using a tapestry needle thread tail through the stitches left on needle and draw up.

EARS

RIGHT EAR

Using 2.75mm straight needles and Yarn A, cast on 44 sts.

Row 1 (WS): Purl.

Row 2: K18, [M1, K1] 5 times, K5, m1r, K3, m1l, K13. (51 sts)

Row 3: P14, m1pl, P3, m1pr, P34. (53 sts)

Row 4: K35, m1r, K3, m1l, K15. (55 sts)

Row 5: Purl.

Row 6: Knit.

Row 7: P15, SSP, P1, P2tog, P35. (53 sts)

Row 8: Knit.

Row 9: P14, SSP, P1, P2tog, P34. (51 sts)

Row 10: Knit.

Row 11: P13, SSP, P1, P2tog, P33. (49 sts)

Row 12: K32, K2tog, K1, SSK, K12. (47 sts)

Row 13: P11, SSP, P1, P2tog, P31. (45 sts)

Row 14: K30, K2tog, K1, SSK, K10. (43 sts)

Row 15: P9, SSP, P1, P2tog, P29. (41 sts)

Row 16: K8, K2tog, K1, SSK, K28. (39 sts)

Row 17: P8, SSP, P1, P2tog, P26. (37 sts)

Row 18: K7, K2tog, K1, SSK, K25. (35 sts)

Row 19: P7, SSP, P1, P2tog, P23. (33 sts)

Row 20: [K6, K2tog, K1, SSK, K5] twice, K1. (29 sts)

Row 21: [P5, SSP, P1, P2tog, P4] twice, P1. (25 sts)

Row 22: [K4, K2tog, K1, SSK, K3] twice, K1. (21 sts)

Row 23: [P3, SSP, P1, P2tog, P2] twice, P1. (17 sts)

Row 24: [K2, K2tog, K1, SSK, K1] twice, K1. (13 sts)

Cut yarn leaving a long tail, using a tapestry needle thread tail through the stitches left on needle and draw up.

LEFT EAR

Using 2.75mm straight needles and Yarn A, cast on 44 sts.

Row 1 (WS): Purl.

Row 2: K13, m1r, K3, m1l, K5, [K1, M1] 5 times, K18. (51 sts)

Row 3: P34, m1pl, P3, m1pr, P14. (53 sts)

Row 4: K15, m1r, K3, m1l, K35. (55 sts)

Row 5: Purl.

Row 6: Knit.

Row 7: P35, SSP, P1, P2tog, P15. (53 sts)

Row 8: Knit.

Row 9: P34, SSP, P1, P2tog, P14. (51 sts)

Row 10: Knit.

Row 11: P33, SSP, P1, P2tog, P13. (49 sts)

Row 12: K12, K2tog, K1, SSK, K32. (47 sts)

Row 13: P31, SSP, P1, P2tog, P11. (45 sts)

Row 14: K10, K2tog, K1, SSK, K30. (43 sts)

Row 15: P29, SSP, P1, P2tog, P9. (41 sts)

Row 16: K28, K2tog, K1, SSK, K8. (39 sts)

Row 17: P26, SSP, P1, P2tog, P8. (37 sts)

Row 18: K25, K2tog, K1, SSK, K7. (35 sts)

Row 19: P23, SSP, P1, P2tog, P7. (33 sts)

Row 20: [K6, K2tog, K1, SSK, K5] twice, K1. (29 sts)

Row 21: [P5, SSP, P1, P2tog, P4] twice, P1. (25 sts)

Row 22: [K4, K2tog, K1, SSK, K3] twice, K1. (21 sts)

Row 23: [P3, SSP, P1, P2tog, P2] twice, P1. (17 sts)

Row 24: [K2, K2tog, K1, SSK, K1] twice, K1. (13 sts)

Cut yarn leaving a long tail, using a tapestry needle thread tail through the stitches left on needle and draw up.

TAIL

Using 2.75mm straight needles and Yarn A, cast on 12 sts.

Row 1 (WS): Purl.

Rows 2-3: Stocking stitch 2 rows.

Row 4: K1, K2tog, K6, SSK, K1. (10 sts)

Rows 5-9: Stocking stitch 5 rows.

Row 10: K1, K2tog, K4, SSK, K1. (8 sts)

Rows 11-17: Stocking stitch 7 rows.

Row 18: K1, K2tog, K2, SSK, K1. (6 sts)

Rows 19-32: Stocking stitch 14 rows.

Row 33: P4, K1, P1.

Row 34: Knit.

Rows 35-38: Rpt last 2 rows, twice more.

Row 39: P1, K1, P2, K1, P1.

Row 40: Knit.

Rows 41-46: Rpt last 2 rows, 3 more times.

Row 47: Knit.

Row 48: Knit.

Cut yarn leaving a long tail, using a tapestry needle thread tail through the stitches left on needle and draw up.

BODY

Work as Standard Body - Plain (see Standard Body Parts).

ARMS

Work as Standard Arms - Plain (see Standard Body Parts).

LEGS

Work as Standard Legs - Plain (see Standard Body Parts).

MAKING UP

Follow the instructions in the techniques section (see Techniques: Making Up Your Animal).

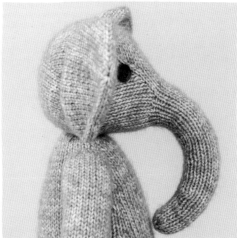

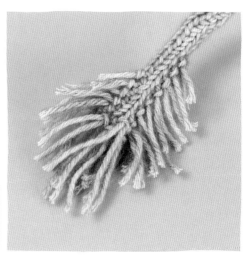

Henry

THE RHINOCEROS

YOU WILL NEED

Please read Tools and Materials at the beginning of the book.

- Scheepjes Stonewashed (50g/130m; 78% cotton/22% acrylic) yarn in the following shades:

  - **Yarn A** *Grey (Smokey Quartz 802), 2 balls.*

  - **Yarn B** *Cream (Moon Stone 801), 1 ball.*

- 2.75mm (US 2) straight needles

- Toy stuffing

- 2 x 10mm (½in) buttons

- Extra strong sewing thread

- Scrap piece of 4-ply yarn for embroidering features

Before you start, please read the Essential Notes at the beginning of this book.

RHINOCEROS PATTERN

HEAD

Using 2.75mm straight needles and Yarn A, cast on 9 sts.

Row 1 (WS): Purl.

Row 2: [K1, M1] 7 times, K2. (16 sts)

Row 3: Purl.

Row 4: K1, M1, [K2, M1] 7 times, K1. (24 sts)

Row 5: Purl.

Row 6: K1, M1, [K3, M1] 7 times, K2. (32 sts)

Row 7: Purl.

Row 8: K1, M1, [K4, M1] 7 times, K3. (40 sts)

Row 9: Purl.

Row 10: K1, M1, [K5, M1] 7 times, K4. (48 sts)

Row 11: Purl.

Row 12: K1, M1, [K6, M1] 7 times, K5. (56 sts)

Row 13: Purl.

Row 14: K1, M1, [K7, M1] 7 times, K6. (64 sts)

Rows 15-24: Stocking stitch 10 rows.

Row 25: P21, P2tog, P18, SSP, P21. (62 sts)

Row 26: K3, [SSK, K1] 6 times, SSK, K16, K2tog, [K1, K2tog] 6 times, K3. (48 sts)

Row 27: P15, P2tog, P14, SSP, P15. (46 sts)

Row 28: K15, SSK, K12, K2tog, K15. (44 sts)

Row 29: Purl.

Row 30: K14, CDD, K10, CDD, K14. (40 sts)

Row 31: Purl.

Row 32: K13, CDD, K8, CDD, K13. (36 sts)

Rows 33-47: Stocking stitch 15 rows.

Row 48 (short row): K26, turn.

Row 49 (short row): YO, P16, turn. (37 sts)

Row 50 (short row): YO, K15, turn. (38 sts)

Row 51 (short row): YO, P14, turn. (39 sts)

Row 52 (short row): YO, K14, K2tog twice, K9, turn. (38 sts)

Row 53 (short row): P25, SSP twice, P9. (36 sts)

Row 54: K8, SSK, K16, K2tog, K8. (34 sts)

Row 55: P8, P2tog, P14, SSP, P8. (32 sts)

Row 56: K8, SSK, K12, K2tog, K8. (30 sts)

Row 57: P8, P2tog, P10, SSP, P8. (28 sts)

Row 58: K8, SSK, K8, K2tog, K8. (26 sts)

Row 59: P8, P2tog, P6, SSP, P8. (24 sts)

Row 60: K2tog 4 times, SSK, K4, K2tog, SSK 4 times. (14 sts)

Row 61: P4, P2tog, P2, SSP, P4. (12 sts)

Row 62: K2tog twice, SSK, K2tog, SSK twice. (6 sts)

Cut yarn leaving a long tail, using a tapestry needle thread tail through the stitches left on needle and draw up.

HORNS

LARGE HORN

Using 2.75mm straight needles and Yarn B, cast on 22 sts.

Row 1 (WS): Purl.

Row 2: K1, SSK, knit to last 3 sts, K2tog, K1. (20 sts)

Rows 3-14: Rpt last 2 rows 6 more times. (8 sts)

Rows 15-17: Stocking stitch 3 rows.

Row 18: K1, SSK, knit to last 3 sts, K2tog, K1. (6 sts)

Rows 19-21: Stocking stitch 3 rows.

Cut yarn leaving a long tail, using a tapestry needle thread tail through the stitches left on needle and draw up.

SMALL HORN

Using 2.75mm straight needles and Yarn B, cast on 16 sts.

Row 1 (WS): Purl.

Row 2: K1, SSK, knit to last 3 sts, K2tog, K1. (14 sts)

Rows 3-8: Rpt last 2 rows 3 more times. (8 sts)

Rows 9-11: Stocking stitch 3 rows.

Cut yarn leaving a long tail, using a tapestry needle thread tail through the stitches left on needle and draw up.

EARS (MAKE 2)

Using 2.75mm straight needles and Yarn A, cast on 16 sts.

Row 1 (WS): Purl.

Rows 2-3: Stocking stitch 2 rows.

Row 4: K4, [m1r, K3, m1l, K2] twice, K2. (20 sts)

Row 5: Purl.

Row 6: K5, m1r, K3, m1l, [K1, M1] 3 times, K1, m1r, K3, m1l, K5. (27 sts)

Rows 7-13: Stocking stitch 7 rows.

Row 14: [K5, K2tog, K1, SSK, K2] twice, K3. (23 sts)

Row 15: Purl.

Row 16: [K4, K2tog, K1, SSK, K1] twice, K3. (19 sts)

Row 17: [P3, SSP, P1, P2tog] twice, P3. (15 sts)

Row 18: K1, [K1, K2tog, K1, SSK] twice, K2. (11 sts)

Row 19: P1, SSP, P1, sl1 kw, SSP, PSSO, P1, P2tog, P1. (7 sts)

Rows 20-21: Stocking stitch 2 rows.

Cut yarn leaving a long tail, using a tapestry needle thread tail through the stitches left on needle and draw up.

TAIL

Using 2.75mm straight needles and Yarn A, cast on 14 sts.

Row 1 (WS): Purl.

Rows 2-3: Stocking stitch 2 rows.

Row 4: K1, K2tog, K8, SSK, K1. (12 sts)

Rows 5-7: Stocking stitch 3 rows.

Row 8: K1, K2tog, K6, SSK, K1. (10 sts)

Rows 9-11: Stocking stitch 3 rows.

Row 12: K1, K2tog, K4, SSK, K1. (8 sts)

Rows 13-17: Stocking stitch 5 rows.

Row 18: K1, K2tog, K2, SSK, K1. (6 sts)

Rows 19-28: Stocking stitch 10 rows.

Row 29: P1, K1, P4.

Row 30: Knit.

Rows 31-32: Rpt last 2 rows, once more.

Row 33: P1, K1, P2, K1, P1.

Row 34: Knit.

Rows 35-38: Rpt last 2 rows, twice more.

Rows 39-40: Knit 2 rows.

Cut yarn leaving a long tail, using a tapestry needle thread tail through the stitches left on needle and draw up.

BODY

Work as Standard Body – Plain (see Standard Body Parts).

ARMS

Work as Standard Arms – Plain (see Standard Body Parts).

LEGS

Work as Standard Legs – Plain (see Standard Body Parts).

MAKING UP

Follow the instructions in the techniques section (see Techniques: Making Up Your Animal).

Isabelle

THE GIRAFFE

YOU WILL NEED

Please read Tools and Materials at the beginning of the book.

- Scheepjes Stonewashed (50g/130m; 78% cotton/22% acrylic) yarn in the following shades:

  - **Yarn A** *Beige (Axinite 831), 2 balls.*

  - **Yarn B** *Dark Brown (Obsidian 829), 1 ball.*

  - **Yarn C** *Brown (Brown Agate 822), 1 ball.*

- 2.75mm (US 2) straight needles

- Toy stuffing

- 2 x 10mm (½in) buttons

- Extra strong sewing thread

- Scrap piece of 4-ply yarn for embroidering features

Before you start, please read the Essential Notes at the beginning of this book.

GIRAFFE PATTERN

HEAD

Using 2.75mm straight needles and Yarn A, cast on 9 sts.

Row 1 (WS): Purl.

Row 2: [K1, M1] 7 times, K2. (16 sts)

Row 3: Purl.

Row 4: K1, M1, [K2, M1] 7 times, K1. (24 sts)

Row 5: Purl.

Row 6: K1, M1, [K3, M1] 7 times, K2. (32 sts)

Row 7: Purl.

Row 8: K1, M1, [K4, M1] 7 times, K3. (40 sts)

Row 9: Purl.

Row 10: K1, M1, [K5, M1] 7 times, K4. (48 sts)

Row 11: Purl.

Row 12: K1, M1, [K6, M1] 7 times, K5. (56 sts)

Row 13: Purl.

Row 14: K1, M1, [K7, M1] 7 times, K6. (64 sts)

Row 15: (A) P27, (C) P10, (A) P27.

Row 16: (A) K26, (C) K12, (A) K26.

Row 17: (A) P26, (C) P12, (A) P26.

Rows 18-20: Rpt last 2 rows, then work row 16 once more.

Row 21: (A) P27, (C) P10, (A) P27.

Row 22: (A) K28, (C) K8, (A) K28.

Row 23: (A) P23, P2tog, P4, (C) P6, (A) P4, SSP, P23. (62 sts)

Row 24: (A) K23, SSK, K3, (C) K6, (A) K3, K2tog, K23. (60 sts)

Row 25: (A) P23, P2tog, P3, (C) P4, (A) P3, SSP, P23. (58 sts)

Row 26: (A) K4, K2tog 6 times, K7, SSK, K2, (C) K4, (A) K2, K2tog, K7, SSK 6 times, K4. (44 sts)

Row 27: (A) P21, (C) P2, (A) P21.

Row 28: (A) K17, SSK, K2, (C) K2, (A) K2, K2tog, K17. (42 sts)

Row 29: (A) P20, (C) P2, (A) P20.

Row 30: (A) K16, CDD, K1, (C) K2, (A) K1, CDD, K16. (38 sts)

Row 31: (A) P18, (C) P2, (A) P18.

Row 22: (A) K18, (C) K2, (A) K18.

Row 33: As row 31.

Row 34: (A) K15, K2tog, K1, (C) K2, (A) K1, SSK, K15. (36 sts)

Row 35: (A) P17, (C) P2, (A) P17.

Row 36: (A) K1, K2tog 3 times, K10, (C) K2, (A) K10, SSK 3 times, K1. (30 sts)

Row 37: (A) P14, (C) P2, (A) P14.

Row 38: (A) K11, K2tog, K1, (C) K2, (A) K1, SSK, K11. (28 sts)

Row 39: (A) P13, (C) P2, (A) P13.

Row 40: (A) K12, (C) K4, (A) K12.

Row 41: (A) P11, (C) P6, (A) P11.

Continue in Yarn C only.

Rows 42-43: Stocking stitch 2 rows.

Row 44: [K1, M1] 3 times, K2, sl1, K16, sl1, K2, [M1, K1] 3 times. (34 sts)

Row 45: Purl.

Row 46: K8, sl1, K16, sl1, K8.

Row 47: Purl.

Rows 48-49: Rpt last 2 rows.

Row 50: K7, CDD, K14, CDD, K7. (30 sts)

Row 51: Purl.

Row 52: K6, CDD, K12, CDD, K6. (26 sts)

Row 53: Purl.

Row 54: K5, CDD, K10, CDD, K5. (22 sts)

Row 55: Purl.

Row 56: K4, CDD, K8, CDD, K4. (18 sts)

Row 57: Purl.

Row 58: K1, K2tog, CDD, K2tog twice, SSK, CDD, SSK, K1. (9 sts)

Cut yarn leaving a long tail, using a tapestry needle thread tail through the stitches left on needle and draw up.

EARS (MAKE 2)

Using 2.75mm straight needles and Yarn A, cast on 20 sts.

Row 1 (WS): (A) P8, (C) P4, (A) P8.

Row 2: (A) K8, (C) [K1, M1] 3 times, K1, (A) K8. (23 sts)

Row 3: (A) P8, (C) P7, (A) P8.

Row 4: (A) K8, (C) K7, (A) K8.

Rows 5-9: Rpt rows 3-4 twice more, then work row 3 once more.

Row 10: (A) K4, K2tog, K2, (C) SSK, K3, K2tog, (A) K2, SSK, K4. (19 sts)

Row 11: (A) P7, (C) P5, (A) P7.

Row 12: (A) K7, (C) K5, (A) K7.

Row 13: As row 11.

Row 14: (A) K3, K2tog, K2, (C) SSK, K1, K2tog, (A) K2, SSK, K3. (15 sts)

Row 15: (A) P6, (C) P3, (A) P6.

Row 16: (A) K6, (C) K3, (A) K6.

Row 17: As row 15.

Row 18: (A) K2, K2tog, K2, (C) sl1 kw, K2tog, PSSO, (A) K2, SSK, K2. (11 sts)

Continue in Yarn A only.

Row 19: Purl.

Row 20: K1, K2tog, K1, sl1 kw, K2tog, PSSO, K1, SSK, K1. (7 sts)

Row 21: Purl.

Cut yarn leaving a long tail, using a tapestry needle thread tail through the stitches left on needle and draw up.

OSSICONE (MAKE 2)

Using 2.75mm straight needles and Yarn B, cast on 6 sts.

Row 1 (WS): Purl.

Rows 2-9: Stocking stitch 8 rows.

Row 10: [K1, M1] 5 times, K1. (11 sts)

Rows 11-13: Stocking stitch 3 rows.

Row 14: K1, K2tog to end. (6 sts)

Cut yarn leaving a long tail, using a tapestry needle thread tail through the stitches left on needle and draw up.

TAIL

Using 2.75mm straight needles and Yarn A, cast on 12 sts.

Row 1 (WS): Purl.

Rows 2-5: Stocking stitch 4 rows.

Row 6: K1, K2tog, K6, SSK, K1. (10 sts)

Rows 7-11: Stocking stitch 5 rows.

Row 12: K1, K2tog, K4, SSK, K1. (8 sts)

Rows 13-19: Stocking stitch 7 rows.

Row 20: K1, K2tog, K2, SSK, K1. (6 sts)

Rows 21-29: Stocking stitch 9 rows.

Change to Yarn B.

Row 30: K1, K2tog, SSK, K1. (4 sts)

Rows 31-36: Knit 7 rows.

Cut yarn leaving a long tail, using a tapestry needle thread tail through the stitches left on needle and draw up.

BODY

The instructions for rows 18-79 are written out below. The Giraffe Body Chart can be used instead of the written instructions if preferred.Using 2.75mm straight needles and Yarn A, cast on 8 sts.

Rows 1-17: Work as rows 1-17 of Standard Body – Plain (see Standard Body Parts).

Row 18: (A) K5, (C) K7, (A) K36, (C) K7, (A) K9.

Row 19: (A) P7, (C) P9, (A) P14, (C) P5, (A) P16, (C) P9, (A) P4.

Row 20: (A) K4, (C) K10, (A) K14, (C) K7, (A) K12, (C) K12, (A) K5.

Row 21: (A) P4, (C) P13, (A) P12, (C) P8, (A) P12, (C) P12, (A) P3.

Row 22: (A) K3, (C) K13, (A) K10, (C) K9, (A) K12, (C) K13, (A) K4.

Row 23: (A) P4, (C) P13, (A) P12, (C) P10, (A) P9, (C) P14, (A) P2.

Row 24: (A) K2, (C) K15, (A) K8, (C) K10, (A) K13, (C) K12, (A) K4.

Row 25: (A) P4, (C) P12, (A) P13, (C) P11, (A) P7, (C) P15, (A) P2.

Row 26: (A) K2, (C) K15, (A) K7, (C) K11, (A) K13, (C) K12, (A) K4.

Row 27: (A) P4, (C) P11, (A) P15, (C) P10, (A) P7, (C) P15, (A) P2.

Row 28: (A) K3, (C) K14, (A) K7, (C) K10, (A) K15, (C) K11, (A) K4.

Row 29: (A) P5, (C) P9, (A) P16, (C) P10, (A) P7, (C) P14, (A) P3.

Row 30: (A) K4, (C) K12, (A) K8, (C) K10, (A) K17, (C) K8, (A) K5.

Row 31: (A) P6, (C) P6, (A) P8, (C) P6, (A) P4, (C) P9, (A) P12, (C) P8, (A) P5.

Row 32: (A) K6, (C) K6, (A) K13, (C) K8, (A) K4, (C) K8, (A) K19.

Row 33: (A) P19, (C) P8, (A) P4, (C) P7, (A) P15, (C) P4, (A) P7.

Row 34: (A) K27, (C) K5, (A) K4, (C) K10, (A) K18.

Row 35: (A) P16, (C) P12, (A) P36.

Row 36: (A) K15, (C) K8, (A) K13, (C) K12, (A) K16.

Row 37: (C) P5, (A) P10, (C) P14, (A) P11, (C) P10, (A) P10, (C) P4.

Row 38: (C) K1, K2tog, K2, (A) K9, (C) K6, CDD, K2, (A) K10, (C) K6, CDD, K5, (A) K8, (C) K4, SSK, K1. (58 sts)

Row 39: (C) P7, (A) P7, (C) P12, (A) P10, (C) P9, (A) P8, (C) P5.

Row 40: (C) K7, (A) K6, (C) K11, (A) K8, (C) K12, (A) K7, (C) K7.

Row 41: (P) P8, (A) P6, (C) P12, (A) P7, (C) P12, (A) P5, (C) P8.

Row 42: (C) K8, (A) K6, (C) K11, (A) K7, (C) K12, (A) K6, (C) K8.

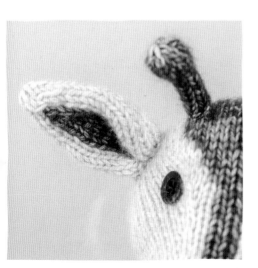

GIRAFFE BODY CHART

Row 43: (C) P8, (A) P7, (C) P10, (A) P7, (C) P12, (A) P6, (C) P8.

Row 44: (C) K8, (A) K6, (C) K12, (A) K7, (C) K9, (A) K8, (C) K8.

Row 45: (C) P7, (A) P11, (C) P7, (A) P7, (C) P11, (A) P7, (C) P8.

Row 46: (C) K8, (A) K7, (C) K11, (A) K8, (C) K5, (A) K12, (C) K7.

Row 47: (C) P7, (A) P25, (C) P10, (A) P8, (C) P8.

Row 48: (C) K1, K2tog, K4, (A) K9, (C) K2, CDD, K4, (A) K12, CDD, K12, (C) K3, SSK, K1. (52 sts)

Row 49: (C) P5, (A) P26, (C) P5, (A) P10, (C) P6.

Row 50: (C) K5, (A) K43, (C) K4.

Rows 51-53: Stocking stitch 3 rows using Yarn A only.

Row 54: (A) K4, (C) K4, (A) K17, (C) K7, (A) K10, (C) K4, (A) K6.

Row 55: (A) P5, (C) P6, (A) P5, (C) P12, (A) P14, (C) P7, (A) P3.

Row 56: (A) K1, K2tog, (C) K9, (A) K4, CDD, K5, (C) K9, CDD, K1, (A) K4, (C) K6, (A) K2, SSK, K1. (46 sts)

Row 57: (A) P3, (C) P7, (A) P4, (C) P12, (A) P8, (C) P10, (A) P2.

Row 58: (A) K2, (C) K10, (A) K8, (C) K12, (A) K4, (C) K7, (A) K3.

Row 59: (A) P3, (C) P7, (A) P3, (C) P14, (A) P7, (C) P9, (A) P3.

Row 60: (A) K3, (C) K9, (A) K7, (C) K14, (A) K3, (C) K7, (A) K3.

Row 61: (A) P3, (C) P6, (A) P4, (C) P14, (A) P7, (C) P8, (A) P4.

Row 62: (A) K1, K2tog, K1, (C) K8, (A) K2, CDD, K2, (C) K10, CDD, K1, (A) K4, (C) K6, (A) SSK, K1. (40 sts)

Row 63: (A) P3, (C) P4, (A) P5, (C) P12, (A) P6, (C) P7, (A) P3.

Row 64: (A) K3, (C) K7, (A) K6, (C) K11, (A) K13.

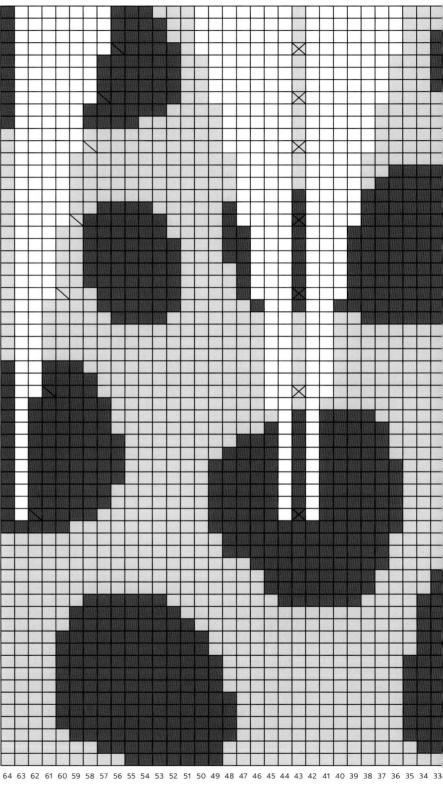

64 63 62 61 60 59 58 57 56 55 54 53 52 51 50 49 48 47 46 45 44 43 42 41 40 39 38 37 36 35 34 33

KEY

☐ Yarn A   ■ Yarn C   ◻ SSK   ◰ K2tog   ⊠ CDD

Row 65: (A) P15, (C) P8, (A) P8, (C) P5, (A) P4.

Row 66: (A) K18, (C) K6, (A) K16.

Use Yarn A only for the next 3 rows.

Row 67: Purl.

Row 68: K1, K2tog, K9, CDD, K10, CDD, K9, SSK, K1. (34 sts)

Row 69: Purl.

Row 70: (A) K12, (C) K4, (A) K13, (C) K5.

Row 71: (C) P7, (A) P10, (C) P7, (A) P9, (C) P1.

Row 72: (C) K1, K2tog, (A) K6, (C) K1, CDD, K4, (A) K4, CDD, K2, (C) K5, SSK, K1. (28 sts)

Row 73: (C) P7, (A) P6, (C) P7, (A) P5, (C) P3.

Row 74: (C) K3, (A) K5, (C) K7, (A) K6, (C) K7.

Row 75: (C) P7, (A) P6, (C) P7, (A) P4, (C) P4.

Row 76: (C) K1, K2tog, K1, (A) K4, (C) CDD, K4, (A) K2, CDD, K1, (C) K4, SSK, K1. (22 sts)

Row 77: (C) P5, (A) P5, (C) P4, (A) P5, (C) P3.

Row 78: (C) K3, (A) K5, (C) K3, (A) K6, (C) K5.

Row 79: (C) P4, (A) P16, (C) P2.

Continue in Yarn A only

Rows 80-85: Stocking stitch 6 rows.

Row 86: K1, K2tog 10 times, K1. (12 sts)

Row 87: Purl.

Cut yarn leaving a long tail, using a tapestry needle thread tail through the stitches left on needle and draw up.

ARMS

Work as Standard Arms – Contrast Hand (see Standard Body Parts).

LEGS

Work as Standard Legs – Contrast Foot (see Standard Body Parts).

MAKING UP

Follow the instructions in the techniques section (see Techniques: Making Up Your Animal).

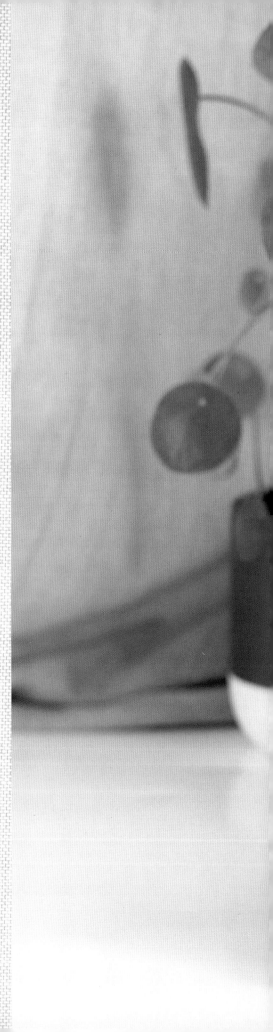

Theo

THE LION

• • • • • • • • • • • • • •

YOU WILL NEED

Please read Tools and Materials at the beginning of the book.

- Scheepjes Stonewashed (50g/130m; 78% cotton/22% acrylic) yarn in the following shades:

  - **Yarn A** *Tan (Yellow Jasper 809), 2 balls.*

  - **Yarn B** *Cream (Moon Stone 801), 1 ball.*

- 2.75mm (US 2) straight needles

- Toy stuffing

- 2 x 10mm (½in) buttons

- Extra strong sewing thread

- Scrap piece of 4-ply yarn for embroidering features

Before you start, please read the Essential Notes at the beginning of this book.

LION PATTERN

HEAD

Using 2.75mm straight needles and Yarn A, cast on 9 sts.

Row 1 (WS): Knit.

Row 2: K1, Kfb 7 times, K1. (16 sts)

Row 3: Knit.

Row 4: [Kfb, K1] 8 times. (24 sts)

Row 5: Knit.

Row 6: K1, [Kfb, K2] 7 times, Kfb, K1. (32 sts)

Row 7: Knit.

Row 8: K2, [Kfb, K3] 7 times, Kfb, K1. (40 sts)

Row 9: Knit.

Row 10: K3, [Kfb, K4] 7 times, Kfb, K1. (48 sts)

Row 11: Knit.

Row 12: K4, [Kfb, K5] 7 times, Kfb, K1. (56 sts)

Row 13: Knit.

Row 14: K5, [Kfb, K6] 7 times, Kfb, K1. (64 sts)

Rows 15-16: Knit 2 rows.

Row 17: P5, K15, P8, K8, P8, K15, P5.

Row 18: Knit.

Rows 19-20: Rpt last 2 rows once more.

Row 21: P5, K54, P5.

Row 22: Knit.

Row 23: P29, K6, P29.

Rows 24-25: Stocking stitch 2 rows.

Row 26: K4, [SSK, K1] 6 times, K1, CDD, K12, CDD, K1, [K1, K2tog] 6 times, K4. (48 sts)

Row 27: (B) P6, (A) P36, (B) P6.

Row 28: (B) K6, (A) [K10, CDD] twice, K10, (B) K6. (44 sts)

Row 29: (B) P6, (A) P32, (B) P6.

Row 30: (B) K6, (A) K9, CDD, K8, CDD, K9, (B) K6. (40 sts)

Row 31: (B) P6, (A) P28, (B) P6.

Row 32: (B) K6, (A) K8, CDD, K6, CDD, K8, (B) K6. (36 sts)

Row 33: (B) P6, (A) P7, SSP, P6, P2tog, P7, (B) P6. (34 sts)

Row 34: (B) K6, (A) K6, K2tog, K6, SSK, K6, (B) K6. (32 sts)

Row 35: (B) P6, (A) P20, (B) P6.

Row 36: (B) K6, (A) [K6, sl1] twice, K6, (B) K6.

Row 37: (B) P6, (A) P20, (B) P6.

Row 38 (short row): (B) K4, turn.

Row 39 (short row): (B) YO, P4, turn. (33 sts)

Row 40 (short row): (B) K4, K2tog, turn. (32 sts)

Row 41 (short row): (B) YO, P5, turn. (33 sts)

Row 42 (short row): (B) K5, K2tog, (A) [K6, sl1] twice, K6, (B) K6. (32 sts)

Row 43 (short row): (B) P4, turn.

Row 44 (short row): (B) YO, K4, turn. (33 sts)

Row 45 (short row): (B) P4, SSP, turn. (32 sts)

Row 46 (short row): (B) YO, K5, turn. (33 sts)

Row 47 (short row): (B) P5, SSP, P4, (A) P12, (B) P10. (32 sts)

Row 48: (B) K5, K2tog, K4, (A) K1, sl1, K6, sl1, K1, (B) K4, SSK, K5. (30 sts)

Row 49: (B) P4, SSP, P4, (A) P10, (B) P4, P2tog, P4. (28 sts)

Row 50: (B) K3, K2tog, K4, (A) K2tog, K6, SSK, (B) K4, SSK, K3. (24 sts)

Row 51: (B) P2, SSP, P4, (A) P8, (B) P4, P2tog, P2. (22 sts)

Continue in Yarn B only.

Row 52: K1, K2tog, K4, SSK twice, K2tog twice, K4, SSK, K1. (16 sts)

Row 53: SSP, P12, P2tog. (14 sts)

Row 54: K1, K2tog twice, SSK, K2tog, SSK twice, K1. (8 sts)

Cut yarn leaving a long tail, using a tapestry needle thread tail through the stitches left on needle and draw up.

EARS (MAKE 2)

Using 2.75mm straight needles and Yarn A, cast on 18 sts.

Row 1 (WS): Purl.

Row 2: K6, [K1, M1] 5 times, K7. (23 sts)

Rows 3-7: Stocking stitch 5 rows.

Row 8: [K4, K2tog, K1, SSK, K1] twice, K3. (19 sts)

Row 9: Purl.

Row 10: [K3, K2tog, K1, SSK] twice, K3. (15 sts)

Cut yarn leaving a long tail, using a tapestry needle thread tail through the stitches left on needle and draw up.

TAIL

Using 2.75mm straight needles and Yarn A, cast on 12 sts.

Row 1 (WS): Purl.

Rows 2-19: Stocking stitch 18 rows.

Row 20: K1, K2tog, K6, SSK, K1. (10sts)

Rows 21-39: Stocking stitch 19 rows.

Row 40: K1, K2tog, K4, SSK, K1. (8sts)

Rows 41-59: Stocking stitch 19 rows.

Rows 60-66: Knit 7 rows.

Cut yarn leaving a long tail, using a tapestry needle thread tail through the stitches left on needle and draw up.

BODY

Work as Standard Body – Plain (see Standard Body Parts).

ARMS

Work as Standard Arms – Plain (see Standard Body Parts).

LEGS

Work as Standard Legs – Contrast Foot Pad (see Standard Body Parts).

MAKING UP

Follow the instructions in the techniques section (see Techniques: Making Up Your Animal).

Charlie

THE CHIMPANZEE

• • • • • • • • • • • • • • • • • • • •

YOU WILL NEED

Please read Tools and Materials at the beginning of the book.

- Scheepjes Stonewashed (50g/130m;
  78% cotton/22% acrylic) yarn
  in the following shades:

  - **Yarn A** *Black (Black Onyx 803), 2 balls.*

  - **Yarn B** *Brown (Boulder Opal 804), 1 ball.*

- 2.75mm (US 2) straight needles

- Toy stuffing

- 2 x 10mm (½in) buttons

- Extra strong sewing thread

- Scrap piece of 4-ply yarn for
  embroidering features

Before you start, please read the Essential Notes at the beginning of this book.

CHIMPANZEE PATTERN

HEAD
Using 2.75mm straight needles and Yarn A, cast on 9 sts.

Row 1 (WS): Purl.

Row 2: [K1, M1] 7 times, K2. (16 sts)

Row 3: Purl.

Row 4: K1, M1, [K2, M1] 7 times, K1. (24 sts)

Row 5: Purl.

Row 6: K1, M1, [K3, M1] 7 times, K2. (32 sts)

Row 7: Purl.

Row 8: K1, M1, [K4, M1] 7 times, K3. (40 sts)

Row 9: Purl.

Row 10: K1, M1, [K5, M1] 7 times, K4. (48 sts)

Row 11: Purl.

Row 12: K1, M1, [K6, M1] 7 times, K5. (56 sts)

Row 13: Purl.

Row 14: K1, M1, [K7, M1] 7 times, K6. (64 sts)

Rows 15-21: Stocking stitch 7 rows.

Row 22: (A) K23, (B) K6, (A) K6, (B) K6, (A) K23.

Row 23: (A) P22, (B) P8, (A) P4, (B) P8, (A) P22.

Row 24: (A) K21, (B) K10, (A) K2, (B) K10, (A) K21.

Row 25: (A) P21, (B) P22, (A) P21.

Row 26: (A) K21, (B) K4, CDD, K8, CDD, K4, (A) K21. (60 sts)

Row 27: (A) P21, (B) P18, (A) P21.

Row 28: (A) K4, [K2tog, K1] 5 times, K2tog, (B) K3, CDD, K6, CDD, K3, (A) SSK, [K1, SSK] 5 times, K4. (44 sts)

Row 29: (A) P15, (B) P14, (A) P15.

Row 30: (A) K15, (B) K2, CDD, K4, CDD, K2, (A) K15. (40 sts)

Row 31: (A) P15, (B) P10, (A) P15.

Row 32: (A) K1, SSK, K12, (B) K1, K2tog, K4, SSK, K1, (A) K12, K2tog, K1. (36 sts)

Continue in Yarn B only.

Rows 33-39: Stocking stitch 7 rows.

Row 40: K8, CDD, K14, CDD, K8. (32 sts)

Row 41: Purl.

Row 42: K7, CDD, K12, CDD, K7. (28 sts)

Row 43: Purl.

Row 44: K6, CDD, K10, CDD, K6. (24 sts)

Row 45: Purl.

Row 46: K1, K2tog twice, CDD, K2tog twice, SSK twice, CDD, SSK twice, K1. (12 sts)

Cut yarn leaving a long tail, using a tapestry needle thread tail through the stitches left on needle and draw up.

EARS (MAKE 2)

Using 2.75mm straight needles and Yarn B, cast on 22 sts.

Row 1 (WS): Purl.

Row 2: K8, [K1, M1] 5 times, K9. (27 sts)

Rows 3-5: Stocking stitch 3 rows.

BODY

Work as standard body – Plain (see Standard Body Parts).

ARMS

Work as standard Arms – Contrast Hands (see Standard Body Parts).

LEGS

Work as standard legs – Contrast Foot (see Standard Body Parts).

MAKING UP

Follow the instructions in the techniques section (see Techniques: Making Up Your Animal).

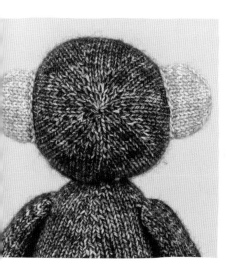

Sophie
THE TIGER

YOU WILL NEED

Please read Tools and Materials at the beginning of the book.

- Scheepjes Stonewashed (50g/130m; 78% cotton/22% acrylic) yarn in the following shades:

  - **Yarn A** *Tan (Yellow Jasper 809), 2 balls.*

  - **Yarn B** *Cream (Moon Stone 801), 1 ball.*

  - **Yarn C** *Black (Black Onyx 803), 1 ball.*

- 2.75mm (US 2) straight needles

- Toy stuffing

- 2 x 10mm (½in) buttons

- Extra strong sewing thread

- Scrap piece of 4-ply yarn for embroidering features

Before you start, please read the Essential Notes at the beginning of this book.

TIGER PATTERN

HEAD

Using 2.75mm straight needles and Yarn A, cast on 9 sts.

Row 1 (WS): Purl.

Row 2: [K1, M1] 7 times, K2. (16 sts)

Row 3: Purl.

Row 4: K1, M1, [K2, M1] 7 times, K1. (24 sts)

Row 5: Purl.

Change to Yarn C.

Row 6: K1, M1, [K3, M1] 7 times, K2. (32 sts)

Row 7: Purl.

Change to Yarn A.

Row 8: K1, M1, [K4, M1] 7 times, K3. (40 sts)

Row 9: Purl.

Row 10: K1, M1, [K5, M1] 7 times, K4. (48 sts)

Row 11: Purl.

Change to Yarn C.

Row 12: K1, M1, [K6, M1] 7 times, K5. (56 sts)

Row 13: Purl.

Change to Yarn A.

Row 14: K1, M1, [K7, M1] 7 times, K6. (64 sts)

Rows 15-17: Stocking stitch 3 rows.

Change to Yarn C.

Rows 18-19: Stocking stitch 2 rows.

Row 20: (B) K15, (A) K16, (C) K2, (A) K16, (B) K15.

Row 21: (B) P3, K12, (A) P16, (C) P2, (A) P16, (B) K12, P3.

Row 22: (B) K15, (A) K14, (C) K6, (A) K14, (B) K15.

Row 23: (B) P3, K12, (A) P14, (C) P6, (A) P14, (B) K12, P3.

Row 24: (C) K21, (A) K10, (C) K2, (A) K10, (C) K21.

Row 25: (C) P21, (A) P10, (C) P2, (A) P10, (C) P21.

Row 26: (B) K4, [SSK, K1] 3 times, (A) [SSK, K1] 3 times, K1, CDD, K5, (C) K2, (A) K5, CDD, K1, [K1, K2tog] 3 times, (B) [K1, K2tog] 3 times, K4. (48 sts)

Row 27: (B) P9, (A) P10, (B) P2, (A) P6, (B) P2, (A) P10, (B) P9.

Row 28: (B) K8, (A) K5, (B) K3, CDD, K2, (A) K6, (B) K2, CDD, K3, (A) K5, (B) K8. (44 sts)

Row 29: (B) P8, (A) P4, (B) P7, (A) P6, (B) P7, (A) P4, (B) P8.

Row 30: (B) K8, (A) K3, (B) K4, CDD, K1, (A) K6, (B) K1, CDD, K4, (A) K3, (B) K8. (40 sts)

Row 31: (B) P8, (A) P3, (B) P6, (A) P6, (B) P6, (A) P3, (B) P8.

Row 32: (B) K8, (A) K3, (B) K3, CDD, (A) K6, (B) CDD, K3, (A) K3, (B) K8. (36 sts)

Row 33: (B) P8, (A) P3, (B) P2, SSP, (A) P6, (B) P2tog, P2, (A) P3, (B) P8. (34 sts)

Row 34: (B) K8, (A) K4, K2tog, K6, SSK, K4, (B) K8. (32 sts)

Row 35: (B) P8, (A) P16, (B) P8.

Row 36: (B) K8, (A) K4, sl1, K6, sl1, K4, (B) K8.

Row 37: (B) P10, (A) P12, (B) P10.

Row 38 (short row): (B) K6, turn.

Row 39 (short row): (B) YO, P6, turn. (33 sts)

Row 40 (short row): (B) K6, K2tog, turn. (32 sts)

Row 41 (short row): (B) YO, P7, turn. (33 sts)

Row 42: (B) K7, K2tog, K3, (A) K1, sl1, K6, sl1, K1, (B) K11. (32 sts)

Row 43 (short row): (B) P6, turn.

Row 44 (short row): (B) YO, K6, turn. (33 sts)

Row 45 (short row): (B) P6, SSP, turn. (32 sts)

Row 46 (short row): (B) YO, K7, turn. (33 sts)

Row 47: (B) P7, SSP, P3, (A) P10, (B) P11. (32 sts)

Row 48: (B) K5, K2tog, K4, (A) K1, sl1, K6, sl1, K1, (B) K4, SSK, K5. (30 sts)

Row 49: (B) P4, SSP, P4, (A) P10, (B) P4, P2tog, P4. (28 sts)

Row 50: (B) K3, K2tog, K4, (A) K2tog, K6, SSK, (B) K4, SSK, K3. (24 sts)

Row 51: (B) P2, SSP, P4, (A) P8, (B) P4, P2tog, P2. (22 sts)

Continue in Yarn B only.

Row 52: K1, K2tog, K4, SSK twice, K2tog twice, K4, SSK, K1. (16 sts)

Row 53: SSP, P12, P2tog. (14 sts)

Row 54: K1, K2tog twice, SSK, K2tog, SSK twice, K1. (8 sts)

Cut yarn leaving a long tail, using a tapestry needle thread tail through the stitches left on needle and draw up.

EARS (MAKE 2)

Using 2.75mm straight needles and Yarn A, cast on 22 sts.

Row 1 (WS): (A) P8, (B) P6, (A) P8.

Row 2: (A) K8, (B) [K1, M1] 5 times, K1, (A) K8. (27 sts)

Row 3: (A) P8, (B) P11, (A) P8.

Row 4: (A) K8, (B) K11, (A) K8.

Row 5: As row 3.

Row 6: (A) K5, K2tog, K1, (B) SSK, K7, K2tog, (A) K1, SSK, K5. (23 sts)

Row 7: (C) P7, (B) P9, (C) P7.

Row 8: (C) K4, K2tog, K1, SSK, (B) K5, (C) K2tog, K1, SSK, K4. (19 sts)

Row 9: (C) P7, (B) P5, (C) P7.

Continue in Yarn C only.

Row 10: [K3, K2tog, K1, SSK] twice, K3. (15 sts)

Cut yarn leaving a long tail, using a tapestry needle thread tail through the stitches left on needle and draw up.

BODY

Using 2.75mm straight needles and Yarn A, cast on 8 sts.

Row 1 (WS): Purl.

Row 2: [K1, M1] to last st, K1. (15 sts)

Work rows 3-42 in a stripe pattern of 2 rows Yarn C and 4 rows Yarn A, starting with 2 rows Yarn C.

Row 3: Purl.

Row 4: [K2, M1] to last st, K1. (22 sts)

Row 5: Purl.

Row 6: [K3, M1] to last st, K1. (29 sts)

Row 7: Purl.

Row 8: [K4, M1] to last st, K1. (36 sts)

Row 9: Purl.

Row 10: [K5, M1] to last st, K1. (43 sts)

Row 11: Purl.

Row 12: [K6, M1] to last st, K1. (50 sts)

Row 13: Purl.

Row 14: [K7, M1] to last st, K1. (57 sts)

Row 15: Purl.

Row 16: [K8, M1] to last st, K1. (64 sts)

Row 17: P20, K10, P4, K10, P20. (The knit stitches on this row mark the leg positions.)

Rows 18-37: Stocking stitch 20 rows.

Row 38: K1, K2tog, K17, CDD, K18, CDD, K17, SSK, K1. (58 sts)

Rows 39-42: Stocking stitch 4 rows.

Row 43: (A) P28, (B) P2, (A) P28.

Row 44: (A) K27, (B) K4, (A) K27.

Row 45: (C) P26, (B) P6, (C) P26.

Row 46: (C) K26, (B) K6, (C) K26.

Row 47: (A) P25, (B) P8, (A) P25.

Row 48: (A) K1, K2tog, K15, CDD, K4, (B) K8, (A) K4, CDD, K15, SSK, K1. (52 sts)

Row 49: (A) P21, (B) P10, (A) P21.

Row 50: (A) K21, (B) K10, (A) K21.

Row 51: (C) P20, (B) P12, (C) P20.

Row 52: (C) K20, (B) K12, (C) K20.

Row 53: (A) P19, (B) P14, (A) P19.

Row 54: (A) K19, (B) K14, (A) K19.

Row 55: As row 53.

Row 56: (A) K1, K2tog, K13, CDD, (B) K14, (A) CDD, K13, SSK, K1. (46 sts)

Row 57: (C) P16, (B) P14, (C) P16.

Row 58: (C) K16, (B) K14, (C) K16.

Row 59: (A) P16, (B) P14, (A) P16.

Row 60: (A) K16, (B) K14, (A) K16.

Row 61: As row 59.

Row 62: (A) K1, K2tog, K11, CDD, (B) K12, (A) CDD, K11, SSK, K1. (40 sts)

Row 63: (C) P14, (B) P12, (C) P14.

Row 64: (C) K14, (B) K12, (C) K14.

Row 65: (A) P14, (B) P12, (A) P14.

Row 66: (A) K14, (B) K12, (A) K14.

Row 67: As row 65.

Row 68: (A) K1, K2tog, K9, CDD, (B) K10, (A) CDD, K9, SSK, K1. (34 sts)

Row 69: (C) P12, (B) P10, (C) P12.

Row 70: (C) K12, (B) K10, (C) K12.

Row 71: (A) P12, (B) P10, (A) P12.

Row 72: (A) K1, K2tog, K7, CDD, (B) K8, (A) CDD, K7, SSK, K1. (28 sts)

Row 73: (A) P10, (B) P8, (A) P10.

Row 74: (A) K10, (B) K8, (A) K10.

Row 75: As row 73.

Row 76: (A) [K1, K2tog] 3 times, K1, (B) [K2tog, K1] twice, K2tog, (A) [K1, K2tog] 3 times, K1. (19 sts)

Continue in Yarn A only

Row 77: Purl.

Row 78: K2tog to last st, K1. (10 sts)

Cut yarn leaving a long tail, using a tapestry needle thread tail through the stitches left on needle and draw up.

TAIL

Using 2.75mm straight needles and Yarn A, cast on 12 sts.

Work rows 1-54 in a stripe pattern of 4 rows Yarn A and 2 rows Yarn C, starting with 4 rows Yarn A.

Row 1 (WS): Purl.

Rows 2-54: Stocking stitch 53 rows.

Work rows 55-78 in a stripe pattern of 4 rows Yarn B and 2 rows Yarn C, starting with 4 rows Yarn B.

Rows 55-78: Stocking stitch 24 rows.

Continue in Yarn C only.

Rows 79-86: Stocking stitch 8 rows.

Cut yarn leaving a long tail, using a tapestry needle thread tail through the stitches left on needle and draw up.

ARMS

Work as standard Arms – Contrast Paws (see Standard Body Parts), except rows 1-36 are worked in a stripe pattern of 4 rows Yarn A and 2 rows Yarn C, starting with 4 rows Yarn A.

LEGS

Work as standard legs – Contrast Foot Pad (see Standard Body Parts), except starting on row 30 work a stripe pattern of 2 rows Yarn C and 4 rows Yarn A, starting with 2 rows of Yarn C.

MAKING UP

Follow the instructions in the techniques section (see Techniques: Making Up Your Animal).

Hugo
THE ZEBRA

YOU WILL NEED

Please read Tools and Materials at the beginning of the book.

- Scheepjes Stonewashed (50g/130m; 78% cotton/22% acrylic) yarn in the following shades:

  - *Yarn A* Black (Black Onyx 803), 2 balls.

  - *Yarn B* Cream (Moon Stone 801), 1 ball.

- 2.75mm (US 2) straight needles

- Toy stuffing

- 2 x 10mm (½in) buttons

- Extra strong sewing thread

- Scrap piece of 4-ply yarn for embroidering features

Before you start, please read the Essential Notes at the beginning of this book.

ZEBRA PATTERN

HEAD

Using 2.75mm straight needles and Yarn A, cast on 9 sts.

Row 1 (WS): K2, P1, K3, P1, K2.

Row 2: [K1, M1] 7 times, K2. (16 sts)

Row 3: K2, P4, K4, P4, K2.

Row 4: K1, M1, [K2, M1] 7 times, K1. (24 sts)

The following rows are worked in a stripe pattern of 2 rows Yarn B and 2 rows Yarn A, starting with Yarn B.

Row 5: K2, P8, K4, P8, K2.

Row 6: K1, M1, [K3, M1] 7 times, K2. (32 sts)

Row 7: K2, P12, K4, P12, K2.

Row 8: K1, M1, [K4, M1] 7 times, K3. (40 sts)

Row 9: K2, P16, K4, P16, K2.

Row 10: K1, M1, [K5, M1] 7 times, K4. (48 sts)

Row 11: K2, P20, K4, P20, K2.

Row 12: K1, M1, [K6, M1] 7 times, K5. (56 sts)

Row 13: K2, P24, K4, P24, K2.

Row 14: K1, M1, [K7, M1] 7 times, K6. (64 sts)

Row 15: K2, P28, K4, P28, K2.

Row 16: Knit.

Row 17: P30, K4, P30.

Row 18: Knit.

Rows 19-22: Rpt last 2 rows twice more.

Rows 23-25: Stocking stitch 3 rows.

Row 26: K4, [SSK, K1] 6 times, SSK, K16, K2tog, [K1, K2tog] 6 times, K4. (50 sts)

Row 27: P16, P2tog, P14, SSP, P16. (48 sts)

Row 28: K16, SSK, K12, K2tog, K16. (46 sts)

Row 29: P16, P2tog, P10, SSP, P16. (44 sts)

Rows 30-31: Stocking stitch 2 rows.

Row 32: K16, SSK, K8, K2tog, K16. (42 sts)

Rows 33-35: Stocking stitch 3 rows.

Row 36: K15, K2tog, K8, SSK, K15. (40 sts)

Rows 37-39: Stocking stitch 3 rows.

Row 40: K14, K2tog, K8, SSK, K14. (38 sts)

Row 41: (B) P15, (A) P8, (B) P15.

Row 42: (B) K15, (A) K8, (B) K15.

Continue in Yarn A only.

Rows 43-51: Stocking stitch 9 rows.

Row 52: [K2, SSK] 4 times, K6, [K2tog, K2] 4 times. (30 sts)

Row 53: Purl.

Row 54: K1, SSK 7 times, K2tog 7 times, K1. (16 sts)

Row 55: Purl.

Row 56: K1, SSK 4 times, K2tog 3 times, K1. (9 sts)

Cut yarn leaving a long tail, using a tapestry needle thread tail through the stitches left on needle and draw up.

Using Yarn B, duplicate stitch (see Techniques: Colourwork) 1 stitch either side of the middle 8 stitches of black on rows 39 and 40 (see photo).

EARS (MAKE 2)

Using 2.75mm straight needles and Yarn B, cast on 16 sts

Row 1 (WS): (B) P6, (A) P4, (B) P6.

Row 2: (B) K6, (A) [K1, M1] 3 times, K1, (B) K6. (19 sts)

Row 3: (B) P6, (A) P7, (B) P6.

Row 4: (B) K6, (A) K7, (B) K6.

Rows 5-9: Rpt rows 3-4 twice more, then work row 3 once more.

Row 10: (B) K3, K2tog, K1, (A) SSK, K3, K2tog, (B) K1, SSK, K3. (15 sts)

Row 11: (B) P5, (A) P5, (B) P5.

Row 12: (B) K2, K2tog, K1, (A) SSK, K1, K2tog, (B) K1, SSK, K2. (11 sts)

Row 13: (B) P4, (A) P3, (B) P4.

Row 14: (B) K1, K2tog, K1, (A) sl1 kw, K2tog, PSSO, (B) K1, SSK, K1. (7 sts)

Continue in Yarn B only.

Row 15: Purl.

Row 16: Knit.

Cut yarn leaving a long tail, using a tapestry needle thread tail through the stitches left on needle and draw up.

TAIL

Using 2.75mm straight needles and Yarn A, cast on 14 sts.

Row 1 (WS): Purl.

The following rows are worked in a stripe pattern of 2 rows Yarn B and 2 rows Yarn A, starting with Yarn B.

Rows 2-3: Stocking stitch 2 rows.

Row 4: K1, K2tog, K8, SSK, K1. (12 sts)

Rows 5-7: Stocking stitch 3 rows.

Row 8: K1, K2tog, K6, SSK, K1. (10 sts)

Rows 9-13: Stocking stitch 5 rows.

Row 14: K1, K2tog, K4, SSK, K1. (8 sts)

Rows 15-21: Stocking stitch 7 rows.

Row 22: K1, K2tog, K2, SSK, K1. (6 sts)

Rows 23-27: Stocking stitch 5 rows.

Continue in Yarn A only.

Rows 28-40: Knit 13 rows.

Cut yarn leaving a long tail, using a tapestry needle thread tail through the stitches left on needle and draw up.

BODY

Work as standard body – Plain (see Standard Body Parts), but work rows 1-76 in a stripe pattern of 2 rows Yarn A and 2 rows Yarn B, starting with Yarn A. Work remainder in Yarn A.

ARMS

Work as standard Arms – Plain (see Standard Body Parts), but work rows 1-40 in a stripe pattern of 2 rows Yarn A and 2 rows Yarn B, starting with Yarn A. Work remainder in Yarn A.

LEGS

Work as standard legs – Plain (see Standard Body Parts), but work rows 21-89 in a stripe pattern of 2 rows Yarn B and 2 rows Yarn A, starting with Yarn B.

MAKING UP

Follow the instructions in the techniques section (see Techniques: Making Up Your Animal).

Edward

THE SLOTH

YOU WILL NEED

*Please read Tools and Materials at the beginning
of the book.*

- Scheepjes Stonewashed (50g/130m;
  78% cotton/22% acrylic) yarn
  in the following shades:

  - **Yarn A** *Pale Brown (Boulder Opal 804), 2 balls.*

  - **Yarn B** *Cream (Moon Stone 801), 1 ball.*

  - **Yarn C** *Brown (Brown Agate 822), 1 ball.*

  - **Yarn D** *Dark Brown (Obsidian 829), 1 ball.*

- 2.75mm (US 2) straight needles

- Toy stuffing

- 2 x 10mm (½in) buttons

- Extra strong sewing thread

- Scrap piece of 4-ply yarn for
  embroidering features

*Before you start, please read the Essential Notes
at the beginning of this book.*

SLOTH PATTERN

HEAD

Using 2.75mm straight needles and Yarn A, cast on 9 sts.

Row 1 (WS): Purl.

Row 2: [K1, M1] 7 times, K2. (16 sts)

Row 3: Purl.

Row 4: K1, M1, [K2, M1] 7 times, K1. (24 sts)

Row 5: Purl.

Row 6: K1, M1, [K3, M1] 7 times, K2. (32 sts)

Row 7: Purl.

Row 8: K1, M1, [K4, M1] 7 times, K3. (40 sts)

Row 9: Purl.

Row 10: K1, M1, [K5, M1] 7 times, K4. (48 sts)

Row 11: Purl.

Row 12: K1, M1, [K6, M1] 7 times, K5. (56 sts)

Row 13: Purl.

Row 14: K1, M1, [K7, M1] 7 times, K6. (64 sts)

Rows 15-20: Stocking stitch 6 rows.

Row 21: (A) P14, (C) P2, (B) P12, (A) P8, (B) P12, (C) P2, (A) P14.

Row 22: (A) K12, (C) K5, (B) K13, (A) K4, (B) K13, (C) K5, (A) K12.

Row 23: (A) P11, (C) P8, (B) P26, (C) P8, (A) P11.

Row 24: (A) K10, (C) K10, (B) K2, SSK, K16, K2tog, K2, (C) K10, (A) K10. (62 sts)

Row 25: (A) P9, (C) P12, (B) P1, P2tog, P14, SSP, P1, (C) P12, (A) P9. (60 sts)

Row 26: (A) K8, (B) K2, (C) K12, (B) SSK, K12, K2tog, (C) K12, (B) K2, (A) K8. (58 sts)

Row 27: (A) P7, (B) P4, (C) P11, (B) P2tog, P10, SSP, (C) P11, (B) P4, (A) P7. (56 sts)

Row 28: (B) K12, (C) K10, (B) SSK, K8, K2tog, (C) K10, (B) K12. (54 sts)

Row 29: (B) P13, (C) P9, (B) P2tog, P6, SSP, (C) P9, (B) P13. (52 sts)

Row 30: (B) [K1, K2tog] 5 times, (C) [K1, K2tog] twice, K1, (B) SSK, K4, K2tog, (C) K1, [SSK, K1] twice, (B) [SSK, K1] 5 times. (36 sts)

Row 31: (B) P10, (C) P4, (B) P8, (C) P4 (B) P10.

Row 32: (B) K11, (C) K2, (B) K1, K2tog, K4, SSK, K1, (C) K2, (B) K11. (34 sts)

Continue in Yarn B only.

Row 33: Purl.

Row 34: K3, K2tog, K8, K2tog, K4, SSK, K8, SSK, K3. (30 sts)

Row 35: Purl.

Row 36: Knit.

Change to Yarn D.

Row 37: Purl.

Row 38: K6, CDD, K12, CDD, K6. (26 sts)

Row 39: Purl.

Row 40: K5, CDD, K10, CDD, K5. (22 sts)

Row 41: Purl.

Row 42: K4, CDD, K8, CDD, K4. (18 sts)

Row 43: Purl.

Row 44: K1, K2tog, CDD, K2tog twice, SSK, CDD, SSK, K1. (9 sts)

Cut yarn leaving a long tail, using a tapestry needle thread tail through the stitches left on needle and draw up.

BODY

Work as standard body – Plain (see Standard Body Parts).

ARMS (MAKE 2)

Using 2.75mm straight needles and Yarn A, cast on 14 sts.

Row 1 (WS): Purl.

Row 2: K1, [M1, K2] 6 times, M1, K1. (21 sts)

Rows 3-65: Stocking stitch 63 rows.

Change to Yarn B.

Row 66: K1 K2tog 4 times, CDD, SSK 4 times, K1. (11 sts)

Rows 67-79: Stocking stitch 13 rows.

Row 80: [K1, SSK, K2tog] twice, K1. (7 sts)

Cut yarn leaving a long tail, using a tapestry needle thread tail through the stitches left on needle and draw up.

LEGS

Work as standard legs – Plain (see Standard Body Parts).

MAKING UP

Follow the instructions in the techniques section (see Techniques: Making Up Your Animal).

Poppy
THE KOALA

YOU WILL NEED

Please read Tools and Materials at the beginning of the book.

- Scheepjes Stonewashed (50g/130m; 78% cotton/22% acrylic) yarn in the following shades:

  - **Yarn A** *Grey (Smokey Quartz 802), 2 balls.*

  - **Yarn B** *Black (Black Onyx 803), 1 ball.*

  - **Yarn C** *Cream (Moon Stone 801), 1 ball.*

  - **Yarn D** *Pink (Rose Quartz 820), 1 ball.*

- 2.75mm (US 2) straight needles

- Toy stuffing

- 2 x 10mm (½in) buttons

- Extra strong sewing thread

- Scrap piece of 4-ply yarn for embroidering features

Before you start, please read the Essential Notes at the beginning of this book.

KOALA PATTERN

HEAD

Using 2.75mm straight needles and Yarn A, cast on 9 sts.

Row 1 (WS): Purl.

Row 2: [K1, M1] 7 times, K2. (16 sts)

Row 3: Purl.

Row 4: K1, M1, [K2, M1] 7 times, K1. (24 sts)

Row 5: Purl.

Row 6: K1, M1, [K3, M1] 7 times, K2. (32 sts)

Row 7: Purl.

Row 8: K1, M1, [K4, M1] 7 times, K3. (40 sts)

Row 9: Purl.

Row 10: K1, M1, [K5, M1] 7 times, K4. (48 sts)

Row 11: Purl.

Row 12: K1, M1, [K6, M1] 7 times, K5. (56 sts)

Row 13: Purl.

Row 14: K1, M1, [K7, M1] 7 times, K6. (64 sts)

Rows 15-23: Stocking stitch 9 rows.

Row 24: K21, SSK, K18, K2tog, K21. (62 sts)

Row 25: (C) P5, (A) P16, P2tog, P16, SSP, P16, (C) P5. (60 sts)

Row 26: (C) K5, (A) K12, (D) K3, (A) K1, SSK, K14, K2tog, K1, (D) K3, (A) K12, (C) K5. (58 sts)

Row 27: (C) P5, (A) P11, (D) P5, (A) P2tog, P12, SSP, (D) P5, (A) P11, (C) P5. (56 sts)

Row 28: (C) K5, (A) K11, (D) K5, (A) SSK, K10, K2tog, (D) K5, (A) K11, (C) K5. (54 sts)

Row 29: (C) P5, (A) P11, (D) P5, (A) P2tog, P8, SSP, (D) P5, (A) P11, (C) P5. (52 sts)

Row 30: (C) K5, (A) K11, (D) K5, (A) SSK, K6, K2tog, (D) K5, (A) K11, (C) K5. (50 sts)

Row 31: (C) P5, (A) P12, (D) P3, (A) P1, P2tog, P4, SSP, P1, (D) P3, (A) P12, (C) P5. (48 sts)

Row 32: (C) K4, (A) [K1, K2tog] 6 times, K4, [SSK, K1] 6 times, (C) K4. (36 sts)

Row 33: (C) P4, (A) P28, (C) P4.

Row 34: (C) K4, (A) K10, K2tog, K4, SSK, K10, (C) K4. (34 sts)

Row 35: (C) P4, (A) P26, (C) P4.

Row 36: (C) K2, K2tog, (A) K9, K2tog, K4, SSK, K9, (C) SSK, K2. (30 sts)

Row 37: (C) P3, (A) P24, (C) P3.

Row 38: (D) K5, (A) K1, CDD, K12, CDD, K1, (D) K5. (26 sts)

Row 39: (D) P5, (A) P16, (D) P5.

Row 40: (D) K5, (A) CDD, K10, CDD, (D) K5. (22 sts)

Row 41: (D) P4, (A) P14, (D) P4.

Row 42: (D) K4, (A) CDD, K8, CDD, (D) K4. (18 sts)

Row 43: (D) P3, (A) P12, (D) P3.

Row 44: (D) K1, K2tog, (A) CDD, K2tog twice, SSK, CDD, (D) SSK, K1. (9 sts)

Cut yarn leaving a long tail, using a tapestry needle thread tail through the stitches left on needle and draw up.

NOSE

Using 2.75mm straight needles and Yarn B, cast on 6 sts.

Row 1 (WS): Purl.

Row 2: K1, m1r, K4, m1l, K1. (8 sts)

Rows 3-5: Stocking stitch 3 rows.

Row 6 (short row): K7, turn.

Row 7 (short row): YO, P6, turn. (9 sts)

Row 8 (short row): YO, K5, turn. (10 sts)

Row 9 (short row): YO, P4, turn. (11 sts)

Row 10 (short row): YO, K4, K2tog twice, turn. (10 sts)

Row 11: P6, SSP twice. (8 sts)

Rows 12-14: Stocking stitch 3 rows.

Row 15: P2tog, P4, SSP. (6 sts)

Cast off.

EARS

RIGHT EAR

Using 2.75mm straight needles and Yarn A, cast on 35 sts.

Row 1 (WS): Purl.

Row 2: K16, [M1, K1] 4 times, K15. (39 sts)

Row 3: Purl.

Row 4: (A) K12, (D) K2, [sl1, K1] 3 times, (C) [sl1, K1] 3 times, K1, (A) K12.

Row 5: (A) P12, (C) P1, [P1, sl1] 3 times, (D) [P1, sl1] 3 times, P2, (A) P12.

Row 6: (A) K8, K2tog, K2, (D) SSK, K6, (C) K5, K2tog, (A) K2, SSK, K8. (35 sts)

Row 7: (A) P11, (C) P6, (D) P7, (A) P11.

Row 8: (A) K11, (D) K8, (C) K5, (A) K11.

Row 9: (A) P11, (C) P5, (D) P8, (A) P11.

Row 10: (A) K7, K2tog, K2, (D) SSK, K9, K2tog, (A) K2, SSK, K7. (31 sts)

Row 11: (A) P10, (D) P11, (A) P10.

Row 12: (A) K6, K2tog, K2, (D) SSK, K7, K2tog, (A) K2, SSK, K6. (27 sts)

Row 13: (A) P9, (D) P9, (A) P9.

Row 14: (A) K5, K2tog, K1, SSK, (D) K7, (A) K2tog, K1, SSK, K5. (23 sts)

Continue in Yarn A only.

Row 15: [P4, SSP, P1, P2tog, P1] twice, P3. (19 sts)

Row 16: [K3, K2tog, K1, SSK] twice, K3. (15 sts)

Cut yarn leaving a long tail, using a tapestry needle thread tail through the stitches left on needle and draw up.

LEFT EAR

Using 2.75mm straight needles and Yarn A, cast on 35 sts.

Row 1 (WS): Purl.

Row 2: K16, [M1, K1] 4 times, K15. (39 sts)

Row 3: Purl.

Row 4: (A) K12, (C) K1, [K1, sl1] 3 times, (D) [K1, sl1] 3 times, K2, (A) K12.

Row 5: (A) P12, (D) P2, [sl1, P1] 3 times, (C) [sl1, P1] 3 times, P1, (A) P12.

Row 6: (A) K8, K2tog, K2, (C) SSK, K5, (D) K6, K2tog, (A) K2, SSK, K8. (35 sts)

Row 7: (A) P11, (D) P7, (C) P6, (A) P11.

Row 8: (A) K11, (C) K5, (D) K8, (A) K11.

Row 9: (A) P11, (D) P8, (C) P5, (A) P11.

Work rows 10 to end as Right Ear.

BODY

Work as Standard Body – Contrast Front 2 (see Standard Body Parts).

ARMS

Work as Standard Arms – Contrast Paws (see Standard Body Parts).

LEGS

Work as Standard Legs – Contrast Foot Pad (see Standard Body Parts).

MAKING UP

Follow the instructions in the techniques section (see Techniques: Making Up Your Animal).

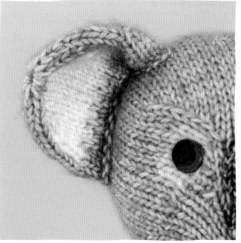

James
THE BEAR

YOU WILL NEED

Please read Tools and Materials at the beginning of the book.

- Scheepjes Stonewashed (50g/130m; 78% cotton/22% acrylic) yarn in the following shades:

  - *Yarn A* Pale Brown (Boulder Opal 804), 2 balls.

  - *Yarn B* Cream (Moon Stone 801), 1 ball.

- 2.75mm (US 2) straight needles

- Toy stuffing

- 2 x 10mm (½in) buttons

- Extra strong sewing thread

- Scrap piece of 4-ply yarn for embroidering features

Before you start, please read the Essential Notes at the beginning of this book.

BEAR PATTERN

HEAD

Using 2.75mm straight needles and Yarn A, cast on 9 sts.

Row 1 (WS): Purl.

Row 2: [K1, M1] 7 times, K2. (16 sts)

Row 3: Purl.

Row 4: K1, M1, [K2, M1] 7 times, K1. (24 sts)

Row 5: Purl.

Row 6: K1, M1, [K3, M1] 7 times, K2. (32 sts)

Row 7: Purl.

Row 8: K1, M1, [K4, M1] 7 times, K3. (40 sts)

Row 9: Purl.

Row 10: K1, M1, [K5, M1] 7 times, K4. (48 sts)

Row 11: Purl.

Row 12: K1, M1, [K6, M1] 7 times, K5. (56 sts)

Row 13: Purl.

Row 14: K1, M1, [K7, M1] 7 times, K6. (64 sts)

Rows 15-25: Stocking stitch 11 rows.

Row 26: K4, [SSK, K1] 6 times, CDD, K14, CDD, [K1, K2tog] 6 times, K4. (48 sts)

Row 27: Purl.

Row 28: K15, CDD, K12, CDD, K15. (44 sts)

Row 29: Purl.

Row 30: K14, CDD, K10, CDD, K14. (40 sts)

Row 31: Purl.

Row 32: K13, CDD, K8, CDD, K13. (36 sts)

Row 33: Purl.

Row 34: K12, CDD, K6, CDD, K12. (32 sts)

Row 35: Purl.

Row 36: K12, sl1, K6, sl1, K12.

Row 37: Purl.

Rows 38-41: Rpt last 2 rows 2 more times.

Row 42: K1, SSK, K8, K2tog, K6, SSK, K8, K2tog, K1. (28 sts)

Row 43: Purl.

Row 44: K1, K2tog 6 times, K2, SSK 6 times, K1. (16 sts)

Row 45: Purl.

Row 46: K2tog 4 times, SSK 4 times. (8 sts)

Cut yarn leaving a long tail, using a tapestry needle thread tail through the stitches left on needle and draw up.

EARS (MAKE 2)

Using 2.75mm straight needles and Yarn A, cast on 18 sts.

Row 1 (WS): Purl.

Row 2: K6, [K1, M1] 5 times, K7. (23 sts)

Rows 3–7: Stocking stitch 5 rows.

Row 8: [K4, K2tog, K1, SSK, K1] twice, K3. (19 sts)

Row 9: Purl.

Row 10: [K3, K2tog, K1, SSK] twice, K3. (15 sts)

Cut yarn leaving a long tail, using a tapestry needle thread tail through the stitches left on needle and draw up.

BODY

Work as Standard Body – Plain (see Standard Body Parts).

ARMS

Work as Standard Arms – Contrast Paws (see Standard Body Parts).

LEGS

Work as Standard Legs – Contrast Foot Pad (see Standard Body Parts).

MAKING UP

Follow the instructions in the techniques section (see Techniques: Making Up Your Animal).

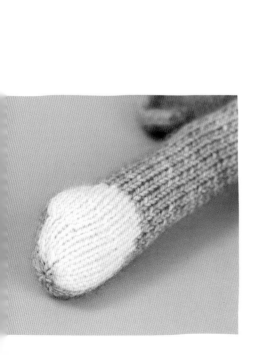

Elsie

THE HIPPOPOTAMUS

•••••••••••••••••••••

YOU WILL NEED

*Please read Tools and Materials at the beginning
of the book.*

• Scheepjes Stonewashed (50g/130m;
 78% cotton/22% acrylic) yarn
 in the following shades:

 - **Yarn A** *Grey (Smokey Quartz 802), 2 balls.*

 - **Yarn B** *Pink (Rose Quartz 820), 1 ball.*

• 2.75mm (US 2) straight needles

• Toy stuffing

• 2 x 10mm (½in) buttons

• Extra strong sewing thread

• Scrap piece of 4-ply yarn for
 embroidering features

*Before you start, please read the Essential Notes
at the beginning of this book.*

HIPPOPOTAMUS PATTERN

HEAD

Using 2.75mm straight needles and Yarn A, cast on 9 sts.

Row 1 (WS): Purl.

Row 2: [K1, M1] 7 times, K2. (16 sts)

Row 3: Purl.

Row 4: K1, M1, [K2, M1] 7 times, K1. (24 sts)

Row 5: Purl.

Row 6: K1, M1, [K3, M1] 7 times, K2. (32 sts)

Row 7: Purl.

Row 8: K1, M1, [K4, M1] 7 times, K3. (40 sts)

Row 9: Purl.

Row 10: K1, M1, [K5, M1] 7 times, K4. (48 sts)

Row 11: Purl.

Row 12: K1, M1, [K6, M1] 7 times, K5. (56 sts)

Row 13: Purl.

Row 14: K1, M1, [K7, M1] 7 times, K6. (64 sts)

Rows 15-24: Stocking stitch 10 rows.

Row 25: P23, P2tog, P14, SSP, P23. (62 sts)

Row 26: K4, [SSK, K1] 6 times, K1, SSK, K12, K2tog, K1, [K1, K2tog] 6 times, K4. (48 sts)

Row 27: P17, P2tog, P10, SSP, P17. (46 sts)

Row 28: K17, SSK, K8, K2tog, K17. (44 sts)

Row 29: Purl.

Row 30: K16, CDD, K6, CDD, K16. (40 sts)

Row 31: Purl.

Row 32: K15, CDD, K4, CDD, K15. (36 sts)

Rows 33-37: Stocking stitch 5 rows.

Row 38: K1, [M1, K2] 3 times, [M1, K1] 4 times, [M1, K2] 7 times, [M1, K1] 4 times, [M1, K2] 3 times, M1, K1. (58 sts)

Rows 39-43: Stocking stitch 5 rows.

Row 44: K1, K2tog, K52, SSK, K1. (56 sts)

Rows 45-49: Stocking stitch 5 rows.

Row 50: [K6, SSK 4 times, K2tog 4 times, K6] twice. (40 sts)

Row 51: Purl.

Row 52: [K6, SSK twice, K2tog twice, K6] twice. (32 sts)

Row 53: Purl.

Row 54: [K6, SSK, K2tog, K6] twice. (28 sts)

Cut yarn leaving a long tail, transfer the first 7 sts onto a dpn, the middle 14 sts onto a second dpn and the last 7 sts onto the opposite end of the first dpn (see photo). Join using Kitchener stitch as follows:

1. Using a tapestry needle threaded with a length of Yarn A, insert through the first stitch on the front dpn purlwise leaving this stitch on the dpn, pull yarn through leaving a tail that you will weave in later.

2. Insert tapestry needle through the first stitch on the back dpn knitwise, pull yarn through leaving this stitch on dpn.

3. Insert tapestry needle through the first stitch on front dpn knitwise, pull yarn through removing stitch from dpn. Insert tapestry needle through the next stitch on front dpn purlwise, pull yarn through leaving this stitch on the dpn.

4. Insert tapestry needle through the first stitch on back dpn purlwise, pull yarn through removing stitch from dpn. Insert tapestry needle through the next stitch on back dpn knitwise, pull yarn through leaving this stitch on the dpn.

Repeat steps 3 and 4 until all sts have been worked.

EARS (MAKE 2)

Using 2.75mm straight needles and Yarn A, cast on 22 sts.

Row 1 (WS): (A) P9, (B) P4, (A) P9.

Row 2: (A) K9, (B) K4, (A) K9.

Row 3: (A) P9, (B) P4, (A) P9.

Row 4: (A) K9, M1, (B) [K1, M1] 3 times, K1, (A) M1, K9. (27 sts)

Row 5: (A) P10, (B) P7, (A) P10.

Row 6: (A) K10, (B) K7, (A) K10

Row 7: (A) P10, (B) P7, (A) P10.

Row 8: (A) K5, K2tog, K1, SSK, (B) K7, (A) K2tog, K1, SSK, K5. (23 sts)

Row 9: (A) P8, (B) P7, (A) P8.

Row 10: (A) K4, K2tog, K1, SSK, (B) K5, (A) K2tog, K1, SSK, K4. (19 sts)

Row 11: (A) P7, (B) P5, (A) P7.

Continue in Yarn A only.

Row 12: [K3, K2tog, K1, SSK] twice, K3. (15 sts)

Cut yarn leaving a long tail, using a tapestry needle thread tail through the stitches left on needle and draw up.

TAIL

Using 2.75mm straight needles and Yarn A, cast on 14 sts.

Row 1 (WS): Purl.

Rows 2-3: Stocking stitch 2 rows.

Row 4: K1, K2tog, K8, SSK, K1. (12 sts)

Rows 5-7: Stocking stitch 3 rows.

Row 8: K1, K2tog, K6, SSK, K1. (10 sts)

Rows 9-11: Stocking stitch 3 rows.

Row 12: K1, K2tog, K4, SSK, K1. (8 sts)

Rows 13-15: Stocking stitch 3 rows.

Row 16: K1, K2tog, K2, SSK, K1. (6 sts)

Rows 17-21: Stocking stitch 5 rows.

Cut yarn leaving a long tail, using a tapestry needle thread tail through the stitches left on needle and draw up.

BODY

Work as Standard Body – Plain (see Standard Body Parts).

ARMS

Work as Standard Arms – Plain (see Standard Body Parts).

LEGS

Work as Standard Legs – Contrast Foot Pad (see Standard Body Parts).

MAKING UP

Follow the instructions in the techniques section (see Techniques: Making Up Your Animal).

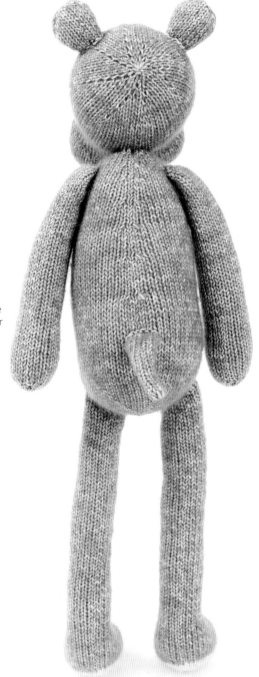

Mia

THE PANDA

· · · · · · · · · · · · · · · · · ·

YOU WILL NEED

Please read Tools and Materials at the beginning of the book.

· Scheepjes Stonewashed (50g/130m;
78% cotton/22% acrylic) yarn
in the following shades:

- *Yarn A* Cream (Moon Stone 801), 1 ball.

- *Yarn B* Black (Black Onyx 803), 1 ball.

· 2.75mm (US 2) straight needles

· Toy stuffing

· 2 x 10mm (½in) buttons

· Extra strong sewing thread

· Scrap piece of 4-ply yarn for
embroidering features

Before you start, please read the Essential Notes at the beginning of this book.

PANDA PATTERN

HEAD

Using 2.75mm straight needles and Yarn A, cast on 9 sts.

Row 1 (WS): Purl.

Row 2: [K1, M1] 7 times, K2. (16 sts)

Row 3: Purl.

Row 4: K1, M1, [K2, M1] 7 times, K1. (24 sts)

Row 5: Purl.

Row 6: K1, M1, [K3, M1] 7 times, K2. (32 sts)

Row 7: Purl.

Row 8: K1, M1, [K4, M1] 7 times, K3. (40 sts)

Row 9: Purl.

Row 10: K1, M1, [K5, M1] 7 times, K4. (48 sts)

Row 11: Purl.

Row 12: K1, M1, [K6, M1] 7 times, K5. (56 sts)

Row 13: Purl.

Row 14: K1, M1, [K7, M1] 7 times, K6. (64 sts)

Rows 15-25: Stocking stitch 11 rows.

Row 26: (A) K4, [SSK, K1] 6 times, CDD, K2, (B) K2, (A) K6, (B) K2, (A) K2, CDD, [K1, K2tog] 6 times, K4. (48 sts)

Row 27: (A) P18, (B) P3, (A) P6, (B) P3, (A) P18.

Row 28: (A) K15, CDD, (B) K4, (A) K4, (B) K4, (A) CDD, K15. (44 sts)

Row 29: (A) P11, (B) P9, (A) P4, (B) P9, (A) P11.

Row 30: (A) K10, (B) K4, CDD, K3, (A) K4, (B) K3, CDD, K4, (A) K10. (40 sts)

Row 31: (A) P10, (B) P8, (A) P4, (B) P8, (A) P10.

Row 32: (A) K10, (B) K3, CDD, K2, (A) K4, (B) K2, CDD, K3, (A) K10. (36 sts)

Row 33: (A) P10, (B) P6, (A) P4, (B) P6, (A) P10.

Row 34: (A) K10, (B) K2, CDD, K1, (A) K4, (B) K1, CDD, K2, (A) K10. (32 sts)

Continue in Yarn A only.

Row 35: Purl.

Row 36: K12, sl1, K6, sl1, K12.

Row 37: Purl.

Rows 38-39: Rpt last 2 rows once more.

Row 40: K1, SSK, K8, K2tog, K6, SSK, K8, K2tog, K1. (28 sts)

Row 41: Purl.

Row 42: K1, SSK, K6, K2tog, K6, SSK, K6, K2tog, K1. (24 sts)

Row 43: Purl.

Row 44: K1, K2tog, K1, SSK 4 times, K2tog 4 times, K1, SSK, K1. (14 sts)

Row 45: Purl.

Row 46: K1, K2tog, SSK twice, K2tog twice, SSK, K1. (8 sts)

Cut yarn leaving a long tail, using a tapestry needle thread tail through the stitches left on needle and draw up.

EARS (MAKE 2)

Using 2.75mm straight needles and Yarn B, cast on 22 sts.

Row 1 (WS): Purl.

Row 2: K8, [K1, M1] 5 times, K9. (27 sts)

Rows 3-5: Stocking stitch 3 rows.

Row 6: [K5, K2tog, K1, SSK, K2] twice, K3. (23 sts)

Row 7: Purl.

Row 8: [K4, K2tog, K1, SSK, K1] twice, K3. (19 sts)

Row 9: Purl.

Row 10: [K3, K2tog, K1, SSK] twice, K3. (15 sts)

Cut yarn leaving a long tail, using a tapestry needle thread tail through the stitches left on needle and draw up.

BODY

Work as Standard Body – Plain (see Standard Body Parts), but work rows 66-79 in Yarn B.

ARMS

Work as Standard Arms - Plain (see Standard Body Parts), but use Yarn B instead of Yarn A.

LEGS

Work as Standard Legs – Plain (see Standard Body Parts), but use Yarn B instead of Yarn A.

MAKING UP

Follow the instructions in the techniques section (see Techniques: Making Up Your Animal).

MAKING UP YOUR ANIMAL

The animals all share common features and techniques in their assembly. In this section you'll find everything you need to know about completing your animal's head, body, arms and legs.

For all the animals please bear the following in mind when assembling their parts:

Where possible use the cast-on/cast-off tails for sewing up. Tie off or weave in any other loose ends as you go.

Use a tapestry needle and mattress stitch (unless otherwise indicated) for sewing up seams.

After sewing parts together bury loose ends inside the body.

BODY

1. Starting at the bottom, thread yarn tail through the cast-on stitches and gather up, then sew edges together stopping about 6cm (2⅜in) up from the centre bottom, but do not fasten off just yet.

2. Now working down from the neck, sew the top half of the back seam together leaving a gap (about 5cm/2in) to push stuffing through.

3. Stuff body (you are aiming for the body to measure about 25cm (10in) around its widest point) and, still working from the top down, close the gap. When you reach the bottom half of the seam, knot both yarn ends securely and bury them inside the body, pulling tightly so the knot goes through to the wrong side of the fabric.

LEGS

TOP OF FOOT

Start by sewing the cast-off edges along the top of the foot together:

1. Using the same yarn as the foot and working from right to left, insert a threaded tapestry needle through the outer loops of the cast-off stitches either side of the centre stitch at the front of the foot, pull yarn through leaving a short tail to weave in (A).

2. Insert needle through outer loop of stitch just worked on right-hand edge and next stitch up on opposite edge, pull yarn through (B).

3. Insert needle through outer loop of next stitch on each edge and pull yarn through (C).

4. Repeat step 3 for each remaining cast-off stitch (D).

5. To finish, working in an anti-clockwise direction insert needle under the 'V' of the next stitch on the right-hand side, centre and left side, then down through the centre seam to wrong side of work (E).

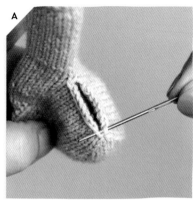

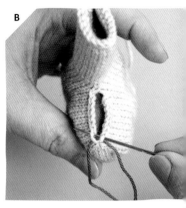

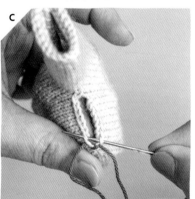

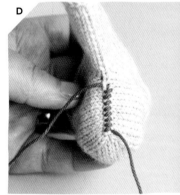

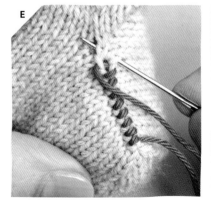

TIP

When stuffing your animal, use small pieces of toy stuffing. Roll and manipulate the body parts in your hands to spread the stuffing evenly and ensure a smooth shape. Tease out lumps using a blunt tapestry needle carefully inserted through the knitting between the stitches.

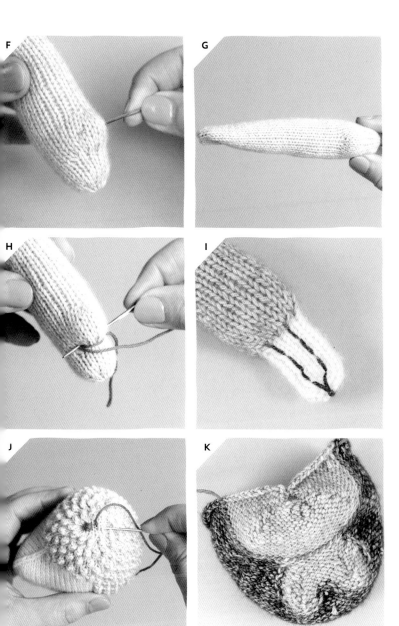

FOOT PAD AND LEGS

1. Sew the bottom edges of the foot together, starting at the front of the foot pad working through to the ankle.

2. Stuff the foot firmly.

3. Sew the leg edges together, stuffing as you go. Only lightly stuff the top part of the legs to enable them to move and dangle nicely.

SEWING THE LEGS TO THE BODY

Matching the top of the legs with the leg position marks on the body and with the leg seam central to the back of the leg, sew the legs to the body using mattress stitch (see Casting On and Stitches). Sew the front half of the legs to the first row of stitches above the position marks and the back half of the legs to the first row immediately below the position marks.

ARMS

For the Sloth – Starting at the gathered end of the claws, sew the side edges of the claws together. To define the claws, embroider 2 lines of stitching using some scrap black yarn, starting at the arm end of the claw and working up to the centre at the other end, then back down to the arm end for the next line (I). On the wrong side of the work sew the bottom edges of the arm/claw together. Sew the side edges of the arm together as below and then follow step 3.

1. Starting at the gathered end of the hand, sew the side edges together, stuffing as you go. Stuff the hand and first ⅓ of the arm quite firmly, shaping the thumb by teasing out the stuffing with a tapestry needle (F). Then gradually decrease the amount of stuffing as you work up the arm, with no stuffing at the very top (G).

2. To define the thumb, sew through the hand and over the top of the thumb a couple of times with a long stitch (H).

3. Sew arms in position on each side of body, roughly 3cm (1¼in) down from centre of neck and with thumbs facing forward.

HEAD

For the Chimpanzee – Using a tapestry needle run a length of extra strong cotton thread through the last row of back loops around the muzzle (K), leaving long tails at both ends. Do not fasten off. Follow the steps below and once you have stuffed the muzzle gently pull the ends of the thread to gather up the muzzle slightly. Fasten off by knotting both ends together and bury inside head before closing seam.

1. Starting at the top, sew edges together, leaving a big enough gap at the bottom to push the stuffing through.

2. Stuff head firmly and close the gap, finish by threading the yarn through the cast-on stitches and draw up.

3. Using scraps of cotton 4-ply yarn, embroider the nose details onto your animal's face (for the animals with a beak or a snout please see Beaks and Snout section). To secure, knot both yarn ends securely and bury them inside the head, pulling tightly so the knot goes through to the wrong side of the fabric.

4. Sew the head to the top of the body using mattress stitch. Roughly match up the increases at the bottom of the head and the decreases at the top of the body and sew together.

For the Ram – Using a few loose stitches, embroider two mini bobbles on top of the ram's head along the seam line to fill the gap (J).

BEAKS AND SNOUT

1. Sew edges of beak/snout together, starting at the drawn up stitches working towards the cast- on edge and making sure any colour changes match up.

2. Stuff beak/snout.

3. Position on face and pin in place.

For the Duck - Match up the top point, side slip stitch detail and bottom seam with the four markers on head (A).

For the Pig - Centralise the snout within the four markers on head, making sure the seam is at the bottom (B).

For the Owl - With seam at the bottom, centralise the beak at the start of the contrast colour of face (C).

4. Sew the beak/snout to face using the Half mattress stitch method (see Techniques: Casting On and Stitches).

KOALA'S NOSE

1. Position the nose centrally with the cast off edge at the bottom and sitting immediately above the line of decreases just above the mouth, pin in place.

2. Sew the nose to the head using mattress stitch method (see Techniques: Casting On and Stitches), lightly stuffing it as you go.

3. Using scraps of cotton 4-ply yarn, embroider the nostril details onto the bottom of the nose. To secure, knot both yarn ends securely and bury them inside the head, pulling tightly so the knot goes through to the wrong side of the fabric.

EYES

1. Using a long sewing needle and a double sewing thread, sew eye buttons in position on either side of head; sew both buttons on at the same time, sewing through the head and pulling them in slightly to indent the face (see main photo of animal in each project for eye position).

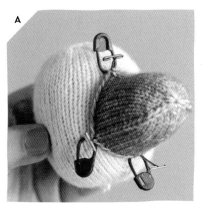

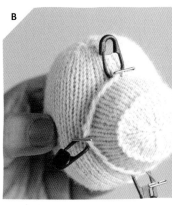

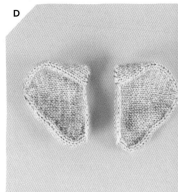

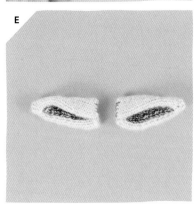

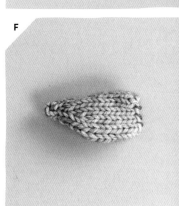

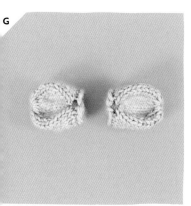

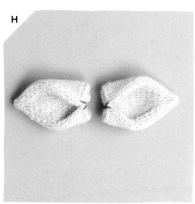

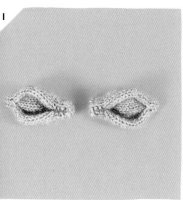

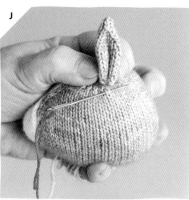

EARS

1. Fold the ears along both lines of decrease stitches so the edges are at the centre back.

2. Sew the edges together, starting at the gathered stitches working down towards the cast-on end.

3. Now follow the instructions below for specific animals. For the other animals go straight to step 4.

For the Elephant and Koala - Lay the ears flat with fronts facing you and the cast on ends facing each other, fold the top 1cm (⅜in) of each ear down (D). Secure with a couple of small stitches. When in place bend the Elephant's ears back slightly to shape.

For the Giraffe and Ram - Lay the ears flat with fronts facing you and the cast on ends facing each other, and then fold the top third of each ear over (E). Over sew the inner cast-on edges together to keep in place.

For the Hare, Horse, Squirrel, Unicorn and Zebra - Fold ears in half with the back on the outside and the front halves touching and over sew the bottom edges together to keep in place (F).

For the Hippopotamus - Fold the two sides of the ear in towards the front centre and join with a couple of stitches (G). Over sew the inner cast-on edges together to keep in place.

For the Pig - Lay the ears flat with fronts facing you and the cast-on ends facing each other, fold the top 2cm (¾in) of each ear down and the bottom 1cm (½in) of each ear up. Secure with a couple of small stitches (H).

For the Rhinoceros - Work as giraffe ears, but also sew the front edges of the ear together for about 1.5cm/⅝in (I). When in place bend back the tip of the ears slightly to shape.

4. Pin ears in place on animal's head (see main photo of animal in project for positions) and sew in place.

For the Horse, Unicorn, Squirrel, Ram and Zebra's ears, take your tapestry needle under the stitches on the head (J) and then right through the bottom of each ear (K).

For the other animals, attach the ears to the head by sewing around the bottom of the ear using the Half mattress stitch method (see Techniques: Casting On and Stitches).

For the Dog - As a final step, fold the ears over and secure the inner front edge of the ear to the face with a stitch about 15mm (⅝in) up from the tip of the ear (L).

HORSE'S MANE

1. Sew the cast-off end of each i-cord into position, along the top and down the seam at the back of the horse's head (A).

2. Thread the loose cast-on tail through the middle of the i-cord and bury inside the head.

UNICORN'S MANE

1. Starting with the shortest first, and in colour order of yarn C, D, E, F and G, sew the cast off end of each i-cord into position, along the centre top and down the centre back of the unicorns head. (B)

2. Weave in the loose cast-on tail through the middle of the i-cord.

RAM'S HORNS

1. Sew the edges of the horn together, starting at the drawn up stitches and working towards the cast-on edge, stuffing as you go.

2. Position horns on each side of the head, pin in place (C and D).

3. Sew onto the head using half mattress stitch (see Techniques: Casting On and Stitches).

4. Gently manipulate the horn so it curls around the ear and secure it to the head with a small stitch (E).

OTHER HORNS AND OSSICONE

1. Sew edges of horn/ossicone together, starting at the drawn up stitches working towards the cast on edge.

2. Stuff horns.

3. Position horns on top of Rhinoceros's nose or Unicorn's head and ossicones on the top of the Giraffe's head and pin in place (see main photo of animal for position).

4. Sew the horn/ossicone to head using the half mattress stitch method (see Techniques: Casting On and Stitches).

MANES AND WHISKERS

See Adding Fringing in Techniques: Casting On and Stitches.

For the Lion - Using the medium lengths of yarn, starting at the centre back of head and working around each row attach the fringing. Trim the fringing around the top of the lion's face and in front of ears slightly to shape.

For the Zebra - Using the medium lengths of yarn, starting at the base of the back of the head and working across each row attach the fringing.

For the Tiger - Using the shorter lengths of yarn, starting at the back of each side of the head and working across each row attach the fringing.

SEWING THE HEAD TO THE BODY

Attach the head to the top of the body using mattress stitch (see Techniques: Casting On and Stitches), sewing around the row of decreases near the top of the body (F).

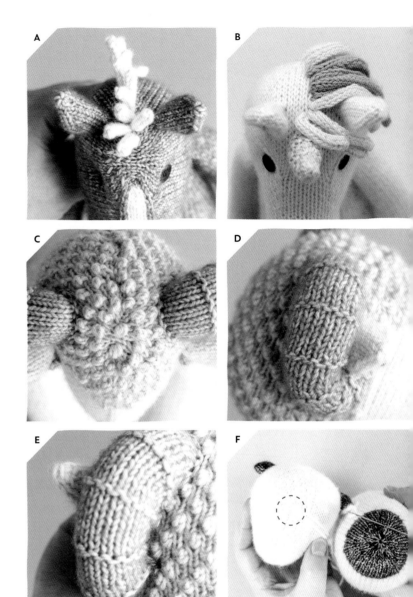

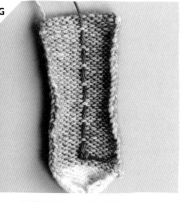

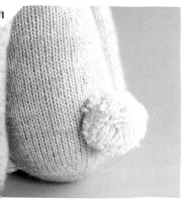

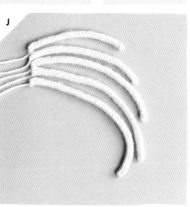

TAILS

CAT, DOG, DUCK, FOX, MOUSE, PIG, RACCOON AND SQUIRREL

1. Sew the edges of the tail together, starting at the drawn up stitches, working towards the cast-on edge and making sure any colour changes match up, stuffing as you go (see instructions below for Cat and Tiger tails).

For Cat and Tiger's tails only – In order to curl the cat's tail slightly, before sewing the edges together secure a long length of matching yarn just above the cream tip. Run this up the centre of the WS, threading it through the back loop of the centre stitch on every 4th row (G) (you don't need to be exact). Poke through to the right side of the tail when you reach the top. Once you have seamed and stuffed the tail, use this thread to draw up and shape the tail, then fasten off securely and bury inside the body.

2. Position the tail on the back of the body, centring it on the back seam and with the centre of the tail 6cm (2⅜in) up from the centre of the gathered cast-on stitches on the underneath of the body; pin in place.

3. Sew the tail onto the body using half mattress stitch (see Techniques: Casting On and Stitches).

4. Add fringing to the Lion, Rhinoceros, Elephant, Zebra and Giraffe's tails (see Techniques: Casting On and Stitches). Use medium lengths of yarn for the Lion, Rhinoceros and Elephant's tails and long lengths for the Zebra and Giraffe's tails. Trim to neaten and shape as desired (H).

HARE

1. Sew the pompom onto the back of the hare's body, centring it on the back seam and with the centre of the pompom 6cm (2⅜in) up from the middle of the gathered cast-on stitches on the underneath of the body (I).

HORSE

1. Starting with the shortest at the top, position the i-cords in size order (I) and sew them together at one end.

2. Stitch the tail to the horse's body, centring it on the back seam and with the centre of the tail 6cm (2⅜in) up from the middle of the gathered cast-on stitches on the underneath of the body.

UNICORN

1. To make sure the tail is in the correct place, start by sewing the two yellow i-cords on to the back of the body, positioning them next to each other (side by side) on the back seam 6cm (2½in) up from the middle of the gathered cast-on stitches underneath the body. (K)

2. Sew the remaining i-cords in place (each coloured pair side by side): pink immediately above the yellow, then peach above the pink, light turquoise immediately below the yellow and turquoise below that.

CASTING ON AND STITCHES

In the following pages I've gathered all the cast-on methods that I use, as well as step-by-step guides to the stitches you'll need to complete your animal toys.

LONG TAIL CAST-ON

(Also known as double cast-on.)

To make sure you have a long enough tail to cast on your stitches, wrap the yarn around the needle the same amount of times as the amount of stitches you need plus about 25cm (10in) extra to use for sewing up later if needed.

1. Make a slip knot (A).

2. With the needle in your right hand, keeping the ball end closest to you, place your left thumb and forefinger between the two strands of yarn. Grasp the loose ends with your other fingers and hold them in your palm (B).

3. Spread your thumb and forefinger apart to make the yarn taut, then move your thumb up towards the tip of the needle, keeping your palm facing forwards (C).

4. Bring the tip of the needle up through the loop on your thumb (D).

5. Then over the top and around the yarn on your forefinger (E).

6. Take the needle back through the thumb loop (insert from top) (F).

7. Gently pull your thumb out and pull on tail ends to tighten the stitch (G).

8. Repeat steps 3-7 (H).

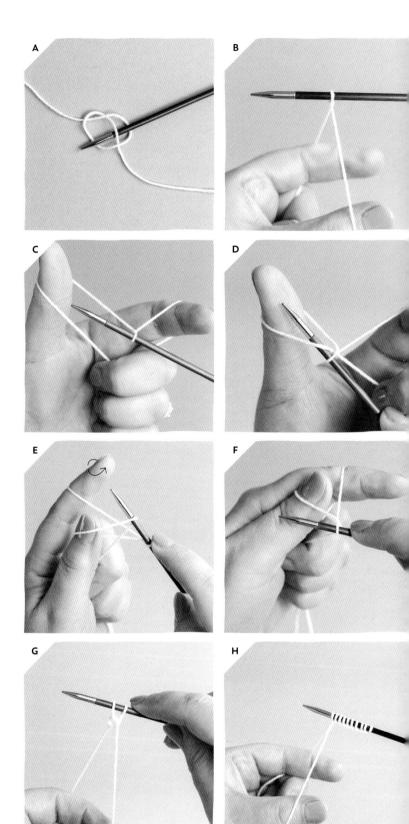

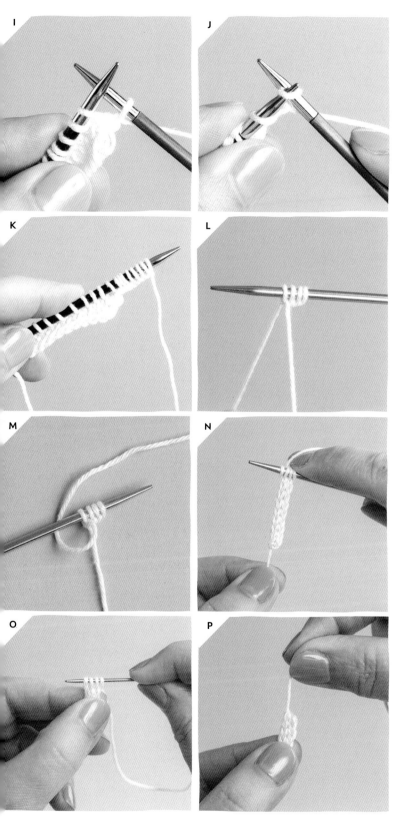

KNIT CAST-ON

1. Insert the right needle into the first stitch on the left needle and knit, but do not take the left-hand stitch off the needle (I).

2. Transfer the loop from the right needle to the left by inserting the left needle up through the bottom of the loop (J).

3. Repeat steps 1 and 2 (K).

MAKING I-CORD

Worked on two double-pointed needles.

1. Cast on the number of stitches needed using Long Tail Cast-On (L).

2. Without turning your work, slide the stitches to the right-hand end of the needle .

3. Bringing the working yarn around the back (M), knit the first stitch, pulling the yarn tight and knit to the end of the row.

4. Repeat steps 2 and 3 until the required length is reached, tugging on the cast-on tail after every row to form into a tube (N).

5. To cast off, cut the yarn and thread the tail end onto a tapestry needle; carefully slide stitches off the knitting needle and working from right to left push tapestry needle with yarn tail through the stitches and draw up (O and P).

Thread the tail (or a length of yarn) onto a tapestry needle. Start with the right sides up and edges side by side.

VERTICAL MATTRESS STITCH

This stitch is used for seaming two selvedge edges together.

1. Insert the needle up through the first cast-on or cast-off loop on the opposite piece, then do the same on the first piece and pull the yarn through (A and B).

2. Take the needle across to the opposite edge again and insert from the front under two horizontal bars in the middle of the outermost stitches (C).

3. Repeat step 2, working back and forth across each side, gently pulling the yarn through to close the seam (D).

HORIZONTAL MATTRESS STITCH

This stitch is used for seaming the cast-on or cast-off edges together.

1. Insert the needle under the 'V' of the first stitch and pull the yarn through (E).

2. Take the needle across to the other edge and do the same with the stitch on that side (F).

3. Repeat steps 1 and 2, working back and forth across each side, gently pulling the yarn through to close the seam (G).

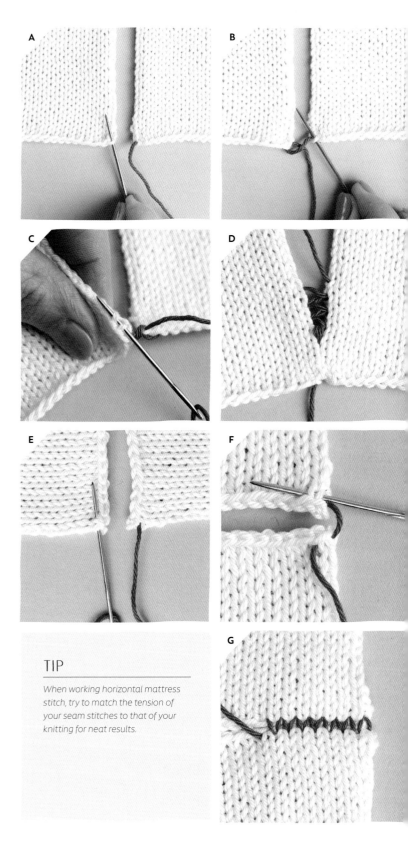

TIP

When working horizontal mattress stitch, try to match the tension of your seam stitches to that of your knitting for neat results.

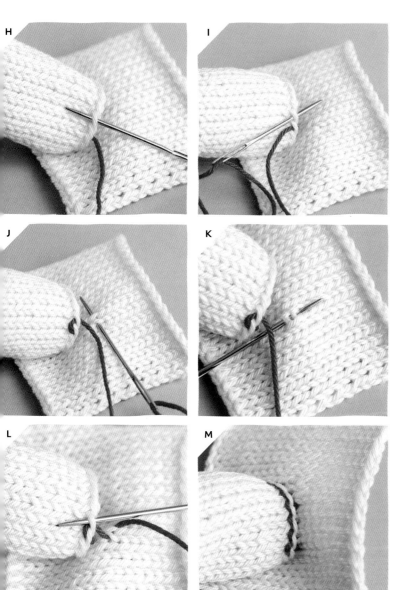

HALF MATTRESS STITCH

This stitch is used for attaching some of the animals' ears, beaks, snout and tails onto the head and body.

1. Thread the tail end (or length of matching yarn) onto a tapestry needle.

2. Insert your needle up through the first cast-on loop of piece you are attaching and pull the yarn through (H).

3. Insert the needle down through the next cast-on loop of the piece and pull the yarn through (I).

4. Insert the needle under the 'V' of the stitch or under two horizontal bars (depending on the direction you are sewing) on the head/body and pull yarn through (J and K).

5. Insert the needle back up the last cast-on loop you worked and pull the yarn through (L).

6. Repeat steps 3-5 (M).

ADDING FRINGING

You will need a piece of card roughly 10 x 7cm (4 x 2¾in) and a 2mm crochet hook.

PREPARING THE YARN

1. Wind the yarn around the card several times (K), use the longer side for long and medium lengths, and the shorter side for short lengths.

2. Pinching the yarn and card between your thumb and fingers to secure, cut through the top loops only for the long lengths, cut through top and bottom loops for the medium and short lengths (A).

Repeat until you think you have enough lengths of yarn.

ATTACHING THE LENGTHS OF YARN TO YOUR WORK

1. Insert the crochet hook through a purl bump from the bottom up..

2. Fold the length of yarn in half to form a loop and holding the cut ends insert the crochet hook through the loop (B).

3. Pull the loop of yarn halfway through the stitch (C).

4. Wrap the two cut ends of yarn around the crochet hook and pull through the loop (D).

5. Pull on both cut ends evenly to tighten (E).

6. Repeat steps 1–5.

BLOCKING

Blocking your work will help to create a flat, neat finish and help stop edges from curling. Use rust-proof pins and leave to dry completely before removing pins. You can use spray blocking or steam blocking with cotton yarn.

SPRAY BLOCKING

Spray the knitted piece with cold water until it is damp but not saturated. Pin flat, and leave to dry completely.

STEAM BLOCKING

Pin the knitted piece flat and hold a steam iron close to the fabric and steam until it is damp (do not touch the fabric with the iron). Leave to dry.

A
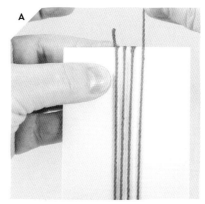

B
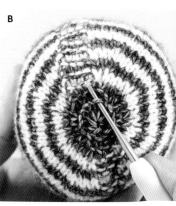

C

D
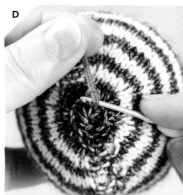

E

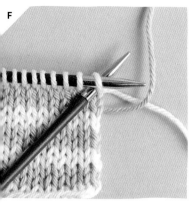

F

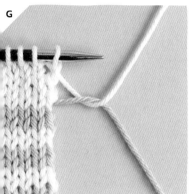

G

COLOURWORK

Some of the animals use colour changing techniques, so I've collected my advice here. You'll find instructions on working stripes and Intarsia, which you will need in order to create some of the animals in this book. But don't worry, colourwork is easier than it looks!

KNITTING CHARTS

Every square in a chart represents a stitch, and these are read in the direction you are knitting if the work is viewed from the right side. When following a chart, work from the bottom to the top and read purl rows (ws) from left to right and knit rows (rs) from right to left.

STRIPES

When working stripes, carry the yarn up the side of the work. Simply drop the old colour at the back of the work and pick up the new colour to work the first stitch (F).

For thicker stripes (more than four rows), catch the old yarn every couple of rows by twisting it with the working yarn (G).

INTARSIA

Intarsia uses separate lengths or balls of yarn for each area of colour (as opposed to yarns being carried at the back of the work). Although, if there is only one stitch between two areas of the same colour, the same length of yarn can be used for both and carried across the back of the single stitch.

It is best to work out how many changes of colour there are before starting and wind the longer lengths of yarn onto separate bobbins or clothes pegs.

An easy way to estimate how much yarn is needed is to count the number of stitches on the chart for each additional yarn length required. Loosely wrap the yarn around your needle once for each stitch then add a further 15cm (6in) for each tail.

To avoid holes between two blocks of colour, work until you need to change colour. Put the needle in the next stitch ready to work it, but pull the old yarn to the left before bringing the new colour yarn up and over it to work the stitch.

SUPPLIERS

BOO-BILOO
www.boobiloo.co.uk

SCHEEPJES
www.scheepjes.com

LOVECRAFTS
www.lovecrafts.com

WOOL WAREHOUSE
www.woolwarehouse.co.uk

DERAMORES
www.deramores.com

THANKS

A big thank you to the team at David and Charles for making this book possible, and to Jane and Lynne for all your hard work.

Thanks also to my family and friends for all your enthusiasm and encouragement, your constant support has been invaluable.

Finally, the biggest thank you has to go to my husband Kevin, who, as always, has been my tower of strength.

ABOUT THE AUTHOR

Louise's love of knitting started when her eldest son came home from school one day saying he wanted to learn how to knit... his interest in knitting lasted about a week, but she has been hooked ever since!

Louise, who has a background in textile design, has developed her own successful brand, Boo-Biloo, selling knitting patterns for toys and dolls. Her work has been featured in various craft and knitting magazines, and in her previous book, *My Knitted Doll*.

To find out more about Louise's work visit her at:

www.boobiloo.co.uk

www.facebook.com/boobiloo

www.instagram.com/boo_biloo

INDEX

A DAVID AND CHARLES BOOK
© David and Charles, Ltd 2023

David and Charles is an imprint of David and Charles, Ltd
Suite A, Tourism House, Pynes Hill, Exeter, EX2 5WS

Text and Designs © Louise Crowther 2023
Layout and Photography © David and Charles, Ltd 2023

This book was first published in the UK and US in 2023
The content in this book was originally published in
Knitted Animal Friends in 2019 and *Knitted Wild Animal
Friends* in 2022.

ISBN-13: 9781446310083 paperback
ISBN-13: 9781446310076 EPUB
ISBN-13: 9781446310366 PDF

This book has been printed on paper from approved
suppliers and made from pulp from sustainable sources.

FSC
www.fsc.org
MIX
Paper from
responsible sources
FSC® C012521

Printed in China through Asia Pacific Offset for:
David and Charles, Ltd
Suite A, Tourism House, Pynes Hill, Exeter, EX2 5WS

10 9 8 7 6 5 4 3 2 1

Publishing Director: Ame Verso
Senior Commissioning Editor: Sarah Callard
Managing Editor: Jeni Chown
Editor: Jessica Cropper
Project Editor: Sam Winkler
Head of Design: Anna Wade
Senior Designer: Sam Staddon
Designer: Blanche Williams
Pre-press Designer: Ali Stark
Art Direction: Laura Woussen
Photography: Jason Jenkins
Production Manager: Beverley Richardson

David and Charles publishes high-quality books on a wide
range of subjects. For more information visit www.
davidandcharles.com.

Share your makes with us on social media using
#dandcbooks and follow us on Facebook and Instagram
by searching for @dandcbooks.

Layout of the digital edition of this book may vary
depending on reader hardware and display settings.